EXPLORING
EUROPE BY CAR

by Patricia and Robert Foulke

Daytrips, Getaway Weekends, and Vacations
in New England

Daytrips, Getaway Weekends, and Vacations
in the Mid-Atlantic States

EXPLORING EUROPE BY CAR

DRIVE YOURSELF TO A GREAT EUROPEAN VACATION!

Patricia and Robert Foulke

A Voyager Book

The Globe Pequot Press

Chester, Connecticut

The color section on international road signs appears courtesy of the United Nations and the International Road Federation.

Library of Congress Cataloging-in-Publication Data

Foulke, Patricia.
    Exploring Europe by car: drive yourself to a great European vacation / Patricia and Robert Foulke. — 1st ed.
          p.   cm.
      "A Voyager book."
      Includes index.
      ISBN 0-87106-230-5
      1. Automobile travel—Europe—Guide-books. 2. Europe—Description and travel—1971– —Guide-books. I. Foulke, Robert, 1930–   . II. Title.
    GV1025.E9F678   1991   91-29080
    914.04'55'9—dc20   CIP

Manufactured in the United States of America
First Edition/First Printing

*To Jopie Been, who for decades,
with map and Dutch guidebook in hand,
has helped us to discover and unravel
the intricacies of Europe*

TABLE OF CONTENTS

Appendix   303

ROUTE PLANNING
MAP OF EUROPE

EDINBURGH

DUBLIN

LONDON

AMSTERDAM

DOVER
PORTSMOUTH
CALAIS
BRUSSELS
FR

BREST LE HAVRE
PARIS

ZURICH
GENE
BORDEAUX
LYON
MILAN
TOULOUSE

NICE

LISBON MADRID BARCELONA

SEVILLE

TANGIER

INTRODUCTION

IT'S NOT SO HARD TO DRIVE IN EUROPE

When we first began driving in Europe more than thirty years ago, we felt we were among the few who had the nerve to order a car and take off. In fact, "taking off" was not quite the right term for what happened as I took delivery of our brand-new little Simca in Paris and eased into the vast swirl of traffic around the Arc de Triomphe. I got in but went around and around, sucked into a maelstrom, until I finally managed to peel off with clenched hands and fearful glances in the rearview mirror.

In those days drivers were encouraged to go through a "breaking-in" period by driving a new car under 35 miles per hour. Poking along alone the next morning before dawn, it seemed to take me forever to reach the ferry to England, then to drive on the left with left-hand steering after reaching Dover. That in itself is not difficult, but it is hard to see around British lorries and coaches to pass unless someone with clear vision is sitting in the right front seat.

It didn't take long for both of us to feel confident wheeling through roundabouts and winding into London for an evening of dinner and the theater. To be honest, driving in England was easier in the sixties than it is today, because there were not so many cars on the roads then, and drivers were more courteous. The pace of modern traffic is just short of frantic in most major cities of the world now, but take comfort: If you can manage New York, Los Angeles, Dallas, or Boston—and have a map showing one-way streets—most cities of Europe will be a breeze.

THE LUXURY OF YOUR OWN WHEELS

In any case, through more years of study and travel we became hooked on driving, convinced that it was (and still is) the best way to see and enjoy Europe. At times when we were living abroad for most of a year, we chose to purchase a car suited to our travel needs: a Simca with reclining seats for sleep when my husband was an impecunious Fulbright scholar, a VW camper when our children were young and we did a lot of camping, a Volvo station wagon when our tall son was too young to drive but needed headroom in the back seat, a Saab picked up in Sweden for a visit with our relatives and a tour of Scandinavia, a VW Jetta to get out of London and enjoy the English country side, and a VW Passat for wide-ranging research on this book. On shorter trips to southern Italy, the Cyclades, Crete, and Turkey, we have rented a variety of small cars that were available locally.

Through all of this experience, we have always enjoyed being in the driver's seat—in full control of decisions about where to stop and what to see or do. We follow no timetables, endure no waiting for stragglers to return to the tour bus, and can alter our day's pattern without worrying about intricate changes in schedule or route. We have been able to get to places well beyond the reach of public transport, such as the little church at the top of a hairpin-curved road above Rapallo, Italy, that had a wonderful collection of votive ship portraits and models painted and carved by sailors grateful for a safe voyage home. We have discovered some of our favorite places by wandering aimlessly, missing a turn, following suggestions from local people met by chance, and simply being open to unexpected opportunities that came our way.

A car provides flexibility, comfort, and privacy. We can stop for lunch when we see an atmospheric pub in an English village or picnic beside a Swiss lake. We can easily reach anywhere we want to stay overnight—from a luxury hotel to a campsite beside a lake. And we can talk, play classical music or jazz on our cassette player, or indulge in a snack while en route.

The view from a train window (if it's clean) can be spectacular, but drivers often are treated to sights only visible out in the country. Images of the Scottish Highlands seen as we wound down through mountains to Glencoe and Loch Linnhe will remain with us. Had we not been driving, we would have missed such amusing curiosities as a road sign in Wales with the longest town name in Britain. Such minor pleasures come by chance, around a curve in the road.

PLAN AHEAD OR TAKE YOUR CHANCES

Of course, motorists may encounter an unusual or not always comfortable driving situation on strange roads—where, no one knows. Sometimes the result is a fiasco, and sometimes it is an experience travelers enjoy recalling and talking about for years. Such moments usually come to us when we have not planned our main route thoroughly enough or are operating on incomplete information.

An auto club in England once routed us through Scandinavia and booked tickets for a ferry back to England from Bergen. As we drove along the main highway from Oslo to Bergen, we were climbing into a blizzard with increasing drifts—in April, no less. Abruptly, we came to a striped barrier across the road and had to turn back. In a nearby restaurant we learned that the main route through the mountains is never open that early in the spring. Since we had booked and paid for a ferry sailing the next morning, our only choice was to drive back to the last railroad town, where the stationmaster agreed to stop a midnight express, load our car onto a flatcar and us into a coach for transport to Bergen. After dinner in the hotel near the station, we dozed in a corner of the lounge until midnight, then drove to the station, watched the loading, and settled into seats to sleep. We woke in predawn twilight to a magical snow scene in high mountain passes, descended to the fjords, and reached Bergen just in time to unload the car and catch the ferry.

Thirty-one years later, in late May, we drove the same road from Oslo to Bergen. As we approached the area where we were turned back in 1960, we found a sign stating that the road was open. On top of the mountain the snow was still there, drifted, dirty, and up to 8 or 10 feet high beside the road. The landscape looked moonlike, with no trees or vegetation. In some windswept areas bare rock supported a few cairns left by hikers. It's a lonely, desolate place with a strange kind of beauty—not easily enjoyed in the winter.

Another time we were not fully aware of the traditional celebrations surrounding Easter in southern Italy. We missed the *autostrada* exit leading to Sorrento just after dark on Good Friday and finally drove into Vico Equense, a town just short of our destination on the Sorrento peninsula. There we met a religious procession blocking the main street. Fascinated by the opportunity, we piled our children out of the car and joined others watching and photographing group after group of silent hooded marchers, each with its own identifying emblem and effigies of figures in the Calvary drama. When we decided it was time to head for Sorrento and set up camp for the night, we encountered another procession coming into town from the other direction. We drove up the hill, hoping to circumvent any other processions, without luck. Marchers were converging toward the cathedral in the center of town along all available roads, with their floats and monks in costume, and they kept coming for hours. Cars and barriers blocked all roads, and everyone but us seemed content to be there for the duration of the ceremonies. When we finally were able to make our way out of town at midnight, torrents of rain descended upon us. We reached our campsite at 1:00 A.M. and struggled to set up three tents in the pouring rain and howling wind. But in the morning, as sunshine dried all of our wet gear, we found ourselves perched on a cliff gazing at Vesuvius across the Bay of Sorrento.

If you explore Europe by car extensively, you are very likely to encounter similar minor misadventures that will jut out as memorable experiences long after the more mundane details of any trip are forgotten. If you've discarded worries about schedules and arrangements, in your decision to travel by car, you probably won't care about the mishaps.

BEATING THE LUGGAGE HASSLE

Anyone who has struggled with luggage through European trains, undergrounds, coaches, and ferry terminals may recall Thoreau's famous image of belongings: a man trudging up the road bent over with all his possessions on his back. Gone are the days of the classic Grand Tour, where servants did all the dirty work. More characteristic is the distress three women friends of ours suffered while traveling from London to Paris by boat-train. Carrying heavy bags, they had to struggle up and down steep narrow steps in the terminals at both ends and inside the ship to make a simple Channel crossing. When we drive on a ferry, all our luggage comes right up the ramp with us, safely locked in the car, and we are immediately free to enjoy sea breezes, have lunch, or read a book.

Whenever we've had problems with luggage in European car travel, it was our own fault. Either we were careless in stuffing our trunk ("boot" to the British) with more gear than we could manage easily, or we violated rule one of car packing: nothing but soft luggage. We blessed the VW camper that served us well for eight months of study, living, and travel as we left it for shipment to the United States in 1968. At that point we struggled through an all-day train trip with five changes to cover a two-hour drive between Emden, Germany, and Meppel, Holland. Kind passengers watched our then-three-year-old, mentally handicapped daughter, who wanted to run beside the live rail as we shifted twenty-two pieces of the year's luggage for our family. Other travelers helped us toss some of our gear out of the windows on very short train stops at each change. We survived.

One of our most successful bouts with possessions, taken abroad for a year of study, was provided by the QE II. It carried home all of our baggage, including books and china, as well as our new Saab. When the ship docked in New York, we loaded everything into the car and drove home. No hassle anywhere.

DRIVING IN LARGE CITIES

The combination of congestion, hurry, and lack of parking makes city driving problematic in many parts of the world. Although we have driven through cities in every country in Europe, the experience can be stressful. Once we were trapped in a Paris intersection that was like a jigsaw puzzle, with seven streets feeding into a small hub. After ten minutes of motionless gridlock, the key driver in the middle of the hub got out of his car, locked it, and walked away in disgust. On another night in the same city, we managed to forget which of the many underground garages we had stashed the car in before taking to the metro. Several of the extremely broad avenues in Naples have no lanes that are observed, so crisscrossing cars produce bedlam. Rome, like a number of other Mediterranean cities, has four rush hours a day, because many commuters go home for the long siesta. Motorists park on the sidewalks there; in many other cities, they will sometimes double-park, leaving their locked cars blocking narrow roads.

Living in London for five months recently, we had time to get comfortable with its driving peculiarities. Since this vast, sprawling city grew from a patchwork of linked villages through centuries, it has many narrow, curved roads and few obvious through routes. But once you know the intricate one-way system and have learned how to dodge the maze of frustrating cul-de-sacs, you can follow the cabbies on well-marked through routes and get across the city quite efficiently. (The one-way map of London is a great help for anyone.) Although the motorway system throughout England is efficient and extensive, it has never penetrated London, terminating instead in a relatively new "orbital" (ring road) that is already outdated and notoriously overloaded, producing "tailbacks" (traffic jams) many miles long. Both on the orbital and within the city, the worst of the traffic occurs during rush hours, 8:30 to 10:00 A.M. and 5:30 to 7:00 P.M., so we soon learned not to drive then. In a country noted for courtesy and self-discipline, we were aghast to find aggressive London drivers (of the eighties, not before) blinking lights or even honking to get us to move over so they could zip by. (Our theory is that younger drivers are not so patient as those who learned to queue during World War II or before.) We also learned to anticipate precariously fast speeds from many other drivers in the city. Whenever we found a good parking space for the day, we preferred to leave the car and take the tube or walk everywhere, especially since car parks (garages) are expensive, and street parking is either metered or restricted to residents in much of London.

Most of the difficulties in city driving come from not knowing your way or being unable to identify streets. Street names sometimes change frequently within a mile, and main arteries often remain unsigned for those on them, even though intersecting streets may be carefully labeled. Our suggestions for navigating in European cities without undue exasperation are:

- make sure you have a detailed, up-to-date city map, preferably indexed, before you start;
- plot your course on the map in advance, making note of one-way streets;
- list the names of streets and numbers of arteries you will use on a "Post-it" note, and stick it on the map;

- if approaching a destination by motorway, mark the exit number you plan to use, because names of intersection roads may appear several times;
- study the city pattern to see if streets are named alphabetically or by some other consistent method;
- learn which sides of the street bear odd and even numbers and discover in which direction they increase or decrease;
- mark the locations of garages and lots in the part of the city you are heading for (often shown on tourist maps with a blue P);
- notice the topography that will help to orient you if you should lose your way (rivers, harbors, hills, major tall buildings, cathedrals, or towers);
- if you drive complicated routes frequently, as we do, set up a convenient map board in the free front seat, either a clipboard for the lap or a large clip mounted on the dash or the lower windshield by suction cup;
- if you have time, make a copy of the pertinent section of your city map, then highlight your route in brilliant color so the navigator can quickly tell the driver where to go;
- when exits are not noticed soon enough, you will not have a prayer of getting into the right lane unless you happen to be there by chance. It's not worth it to abruptly change lanes and perhaps cause an accident. Better to get off at the next exit and return.

Then drive carefully with the flow; if the traffic moves too fast for comfort, use the right lane (left lane in Britain). Become aware of the bad driving habits of the city—sometimes drivers disregard red lights completely or honk their horns incessantly—but don't imitate them. When you reach the section of the city you want to explore, head for a parking place. You'll see a lot more of the city by walking anyway.

MOTORWAYS, AUTOBAHNS, AUTOROUTES, AND AUTOSTRADAS

European networks of superhighways are extensive and sophisticated, allowing motorists to cover large distances in short times. Some (but not all) provide easy access to major cities, and most have very clear signing and excellent service facilities. (One immaculate service center we stopped at in the Netherlands had several shops and three restaurants, offering everything from fast food to full candle-lit dinners.) But, in a curious reversal of expectations, American drivers accustomed to a leisurely 55 to 65 mph must get used to almost-unlimited speeds on expressways that live up to their name. Stories about Mercedes drivers cruising the passing lanes of autobahns and blinking their headlights from half a mile behind are old saws but true. Be prepared to move over quickly to let through a car that may be clocking 120 mph. Although some superhighways have nominal speed limits, say of 75 mph/120 kph, they are generally ignored in the fast lanes. Even the middle or slow lanes on some motorways in Britain move along between 70 and 80 mph. To make matters worse, tailgating is just as rampant in Europe as it is in the States—and far more dangerous at higher speeds. We avoid white-knuckle driving by monitoring all three rearview mirrors constantly so we know what is about to happen around us. These same motorways can become long parking lots during commuting hours or holiday weekends. When the congestion gets too much to tolerate, we simply leave the highway and take off on country roads.

WE CAN'T WAIT
TO HIT THE ROAD AGAIN

In our experience, European cities can usually be navigated without incident, and motorways increase the range of exploration, but driving in the country is what it's all about. There the pace is slower and travelers can move about at leisure. International road signs are used everywhere, and country drivers seem to be courteous even when you've misinterpreted a sign. Here are a few hints that will add to your enjoyment. Get a good detailed regional map, such as a Michelin, that will help you think about the topography, gradients on roads, and altitude. Allow extra driving time, both for winding roads through mountains and along fjords as well as for beautiful but slow secondary roads, one-lane bridges, detours, and other natural obstacles to speed. That will allow you time to enjoy extra stops and the feeling of leisure they bring. Even getting lost may lead to a pleasing unexpected discovery. The sights and sounds of a trip meandering through the countryside will put smiles on your faces, and when local people respond to those smiles, you may find new friends.

PLANNING YOUR DRIVING VACATION

After many years of figuring out driving details for ourselves, we began sharing the results of our research and experience with friends. Not that we know it all—far from it—but many successful trips have given us confidence in planning European journeys by car. The first part of this book deals with that pretrip planning process—formulating an itinerary and then making arrangements to rent, lease, or buy a car—and includes an alphabetized compendium of tips for the road.

The rest of the book treats each country in Europe separately. Each of the chapters includes a topographical sketch to give you some idea of how that country's mountains, rivers, plains, and so on impede or improve road travel. Beyond that, we have gathered detailed practical information not found outside of the handfuls of brochures scattered about various agencies and bureaus. We have written to and called all of them, looking for information to supplement our own driving experience in every country included here. Highway information, road conditions, driving regulations, special signing, parking rules, and any unusual legal or equipment requirements are specified for each country. We suggest ways of planning routes, details to check or look out for along the way, and how topography and driving conditions can determine realistic planning of your time. As an aid to this process, the book includes a generous supply of maps for planning and orientation: an overall map of each country's main highway system and many individual maps indicating the approaches into major cities. (These are intended only to orient you; to drive successfully, you will want to buy more detailed maps for the countries and cities you visit.)

OBTAINING CURRENT INFORMATION

We have chosen not to include precise details on certain subjects if the information is likely to change after we go to press; some information on car rental (the collision damage waiver, for example) changes constantly. The doors of Eastern Europe have been opened so recently that there will surely be changes in requirements and other details. But we include the latest wrinkles we know of and suggest that close to your time of departure you obtain the final update on insurance costs, rental costs, border regulations, and required documents to help insure a rewarding trip.

PART I:

PRETRIP PLANNING

A riverside campsite provides entertainment for many in the Ardennes hills of Luxembourg. (Luxembourg Travel Office/Jean Proess)

WHY YOU NEED
AN ITINERARY

If you're attracted to the idea of exploring Europe by car for its freedom from daily schedules, railroad timetables, fixed hotel reservations, and the like, then why do you need an itinerary at all? An itinerary provides a framework for your trip, so you won't get trapped into driving tediously long days, skipping places you wanted to see, or being surprised by difficult road conditions. We believe in flexibility, but it makes sense to look ahead down the road you will travel to make your days run smoothly.

Building an itinerary is one of the best ways to prepare for the imaginative pleasures as well as the pragmatics of a trip. First you will want to immerse yourself in some general reading about the cities or regions that particularly intrigue you and satisfy your interests. These might include a special focus such as Gothic cathedrals, English country houses and gardens, castles on the Rhine, French wine-growing regions, Moorish culture in Spain, Renaissance art in Italy, the musical heritage of Austria, Norwegian fjords, or mountain hiking in the Swiss Alps. Next you will want to select an airport of entry and calculate the scope of your travels in the time you have available. Some of our friends prefer grand sweeps, others more intense or more leisurely smaller circuits. If you have never been to Italy, you may want to plunge from the lake district right down the spine of the Apennines, visiting half a dozen of the most remarkable cities in Europe; alternatively, you might choose to spend the same number of days in the hill towns of Umbria and Tuscany.

Like most worthwhile forms of human activity, travel has its range of styles, and you will want to find one that suits your temperament and satisfies your desires. Will you drive a whole day to reach a destination and then settle down for two or three? Or will you keep moving but drive no more than half a day's worth, puttering about as you go? Will you enjoy local cuisine in leisurely lunch stops or just picnic on local bread, wine, and cheese? Do you require a fairly firm idea of where you will spend the night, or are you comfortable with taking your chances on finding accommodations as you go? And how much leeway will you allow for changing your plans in response to weather, opportunity, energy, or simple inclination? The fact that you should answer all these questions before building a personal itinerary precludes set patterns. Therefore you will find no canned tourist itineraries in this book.

But we can offer you some advice on how to create an itinerary suited to your own style. Each country in this book has a section on topography describing the kind of terrain you will be passing through. By knowing something about general conditions, you can make a rough estimate of the time it will take to cover the distance between stops and thereby devise a tentative daily plan. When zooming along a motorway in England, you can usually count on driving at least 60 miles in 60 minutes; but when traveling in the mountains or on secondary roads, you may need to double that time. In the sample itineraries that follow, for example, we have estimated three hours for 295 km (179 mi) of motorway driving between Vienna and Prague and five hours for the same distance between Zurich and Milan, also on motorways but with mountain curves and tunnels. In some areas, where the going is very slow, another percentage should be added: From direct experience of beautiful but rough-surfaced Irish roads, we know that it takes 2¾ hours to drive the 78 miles from Waterford to Cork comfortably and nearly an hour to swerve through a mere 26 km (16 mi) of corniche between Sorrento and Positano on the Amalfi Drive.

There are several easy ways to estimate mileage. If you don't need the precision of adding up all the miles between towns on a reliable map, you can use the distance tables printed on some; the AAA regional planning maps have useful tables that include somewhat conservative time estimates. Or you can buy one of the little "map route measurers" that roll along a map while a wheel measures the distance in centimeters. To figure distance in mileage or kilometers, just roll the wheel backward to zero along the appropriate scale printed on the map. It really does work well enough to provide you with a rough number for planning. (Curvy mountain roads require a certain amount of guesswork, as the wheel cannot make all of those turns on a small map.)

We have found it convenient either to transfer the distances and times for an itinerary onto an index card or to print them out by computer. The appendixes contain an Itinerary Guide sheet that can be torn out to use for your next trip. Here are some sample itineraries from our recent European travels.

Little England

This is a ten-day loop trip in the English countryside from Cambridge to Stratford, Warwick, Kenilworth, Stow-on-the-Wold, Oxford and Woodstock, Bath, Salisbury, Portsmouth, Brighton, and Canterbury and back to Cambridge. This circuit was designed to show visiting relatives a good slice of England—university and cathedral towns, towns renowned for other reasons, castles and country houses, the Cotswolds, and a taste of the sea. It could easily be appended to a stay in London.

Day(s)	Miles	Hours	City
1–2	92	2:20	Warwick, Kenilworth,
	34	:45	Stratford, Stow-on-the-Wold
3–4	27	:30	Oxford and Woodstock
5–6	66	1:20	Bath
	39	:50	Salisbury
7	43	1:00	Portsmouth
8	54	1:10	Brighton
9	80	1:45	Canterbury
10	113	2:00	Cambridge

An Irish circuit

This eleven-day trip around Ireland should have been longer to eliminate tiring one-night stands. Another time we will pick several locations, particularly in the southwest, and settle in for a few nights. Driving is much slower in Ireland than in England, so we estimated double the normal time to cover distances. The circuit begins and ends in the ferry port of Rosslare.

Day(s)	Miles	Hours	City
1	50	1:40	Waterford
2	78	2:40	Cork
3	49	1:20	Bantry
4	18	:40	Kenmare
5	17	:35	Killarney
6	69	2:20	Limerick
7	65	2:10	Galway
8	55	1:50	Westport
9–10	140	4:40	Dublin
11	80	2:40	Rosslare

Swooping South

Our sixteen-day one-way trip from Britain took us through Germany, Switzerland, and Italy. (Please note that kilometers and hours do not always appear to be consistent because we have allowed for mountains and other slow road conditions.) If the appropriate car pickups and drops can be arranged, fly-drive trips of this kind are very useful for travelers long on ambition but short on time. This trip began on a Channel ferry heading for Vlissingen but could have started just as well from the airport in Amsterdam or Brussels.

Days	Kilo-meters	Hours	City
1–2	500	5:00	Cologne and Koblenz
3–4	225	2:30	Freiburg and the Black Forest
5–6	172	2:30	Lucerne
7–8	230	3:30	Como
9–10	306	3:00	Venice
11–12	240	2:30	Florence
13–14	270	3:00	Rome
15–16	205	2:00	Naples and Capri

The following itineraries give you some idea as to the driving times between popular destinations in three additional areas on the continent:

Central Europe

Days	Kilometers	Hours	City
1–3			Budapest
4–6	240	4:00	Vienna
7–9	295	4:00	Prague
10–12	330	4:30	Berlin

Scandinavia

Days	Kilometers	Hours	City
1–3			Copenhagen
4–6	525	7:30 plus ferry	Stockholm
7–9	531	8:00	Oslo
10–12	495	8:30	Bergen

Benelux and France

Day(s)	Kilo-meters	Hours	City
1–3			Amsterdam
4–5	55	:40	The Hague/Leiden
6–8	175	2:30	Brussels
9	45	:50	Ghent
10	46	:50	Bruges
11–13	300	3:30	Paris
14–15	230	2:30	Tours

RENT, LEASE, OR BUY?

With a tentative itinerary in mind, you should next decide how to get your wheels. Renting, leasing, and buying each have advantages and disadvantages, so your circumstances and the focus and length of the trip will swing the balance. For trips of less than three weeks, rental with pickup and drop-off at the airport is usually the most convenient arrangement, unless you have special requirements for vehicle size and equipment. If you are traveling with a number of children or a group of friends, or camping, you may want a van or other equipment not always available at airport rental agencies. In those cases, or when your stay will be extended to a month or more, leasing may be more practical and less expensive, and there could be tax benefits if your trip is linked to business travel.

The final option—ordering a new car for European delivery—is still very attractive if you want or need a European car. Although the savings on list price are not as great as they were a decade ago, they are still substantial (especially for higher-priced cars), and there are additional advantages. Under the diplomat and tourist delivery schemes of most European manufacturers, you will pay none of the commonly added European car taxes nor VAT (Value-Added Tax), which can add as much as 40 percent to the cost of a car, as long as you export the car from Europe within one year. Many European manufacturers will also ship the car home free, either to a port of entry or all the way to your local dealer. So for long trips or extended residence, the advantages of car purchase are threefold: lower initial cost, reduced customs and sales taxes, and, most important, cheaper transportation abroad.

CAR RENTAL

As a general rule we like to order rental cars before leaving home. The rates are often better, and there is time to shop around if the first several quotes seem too high. You can also methodically work down your own checklist of requirements to make sure the deal is right. If you wait until you reach the airport rental agencies, you may be forced to take what they have, often with some undesirable or expensive options, or even draw a blank, especially during high tourist season. And after a long flight, most of us are short on patience for long lines and not alert enough to decode the fine print of rental agreements.

Although airport rental cars are likely to be relatively new and reliable, the same cannot be said of casual pickups. When we were traveling by boat in the Mediterranean one summer and couldn't book our occasional rental cars in advance, we had no choice but to walk from the dock to perhaps the only agency in a seaport town. On Crete the car we rented turned balky and refused to drive any farther when we were halfway up a remote mountain on a single-track dirt road. After hiking the rest of the way to the archaeological site and returning, we had to back half a mile down to the nearest turnaround, then jump start the car again by pushing it down the rutty mountain track. Several of the other cars we rented that summer had their own peculiarities, but none failed us in such dramatic circumstances.

Many rental cars in Europe are smaller than Americans are used to. Although it is possible to rent a midsize or luxury car (if you are willing to pay for it!), many Europeans stick by the minis, especially for short hauls, because they easily nip around obstacles on narrow city streets and tuck into tiny parking spaces. Also, they consume far less gasoline than even a modest compact, and gasoline is exorbitantly expensive in Europe, at least by American standards. (Europeans marvel at the reluctance of

American congressmen to solve budge deficits by doubling or tripling gasoline taxes.)

But if you go for a very small rental car, remember the size of the people you will want to cram into a very small space, particularly in the back (semi)seat, if there is one; and keep in mind that prisoners do not wear well as touring companions. And then there is luggage: a mini's trunk will just about hold what three or four people can stuff under an airline seat, no more. If you are traveling heavier than that, move to a midsize rental, and even then warn everyone to think soft. Hard luggage is about as welcome in a car as in a boat, because it cannot be stowed easily, if at all. Other reminders for Americans: Air conditioning is not the norm because it is not needed in much of Europe; stick shifts are more common than automatics (for which you will pay a premium); baby seats and car racks are not always available and need to be booked ahead. If you are headed for major cities, particularly in southern Europe, balance the convenience of a hatchback or station wagon against the exposure of luggage to waiting thieves.

When you have decided what kind of car suits your needs, it almost always pays to spend some time shopping for rates. Since the cost of renting a car can vary considerably with location, you may want to consider starting your trip in countries with lower rates. But there are many factors to consider before making such a decision. Getting to some lower-rate areas may cost more because you can't take advantage of long direct flights with special reduced airfares. Some high-rate countries tend to have lower Value-Added Taxes, and some with lower rates will not offer the same flexibility in pickup and drop-off points or will levy exorbitant charges if you drop off your car a thousand miles and several borders distant from where you picked it up. Although such conditions may change, the changes are likely to be uneven, so it is always wise to ask about the availability and cost of several prospective drop points before you book. Also think about any limits or changes in insurance coverage when you drive a rental car across borders, but that is only a piece of the larger insurance problem.

Taxes on Car Rentals

Although it isn't easy to figure out the various government taxes you will pay on car rentals in each country, the current ratio at press time can be useful. Bear in mind that these are bound to change and ask when you are making your plans.

Austria 21.2%
Belgium 25%
Czechoslovakia 15%
Denmark 22%
Finland 19.76%
France 22%
Germany 14%
Greece 16%
Hungary 25%
Ireland 10% Groups A-I;
   25% Group K

Italy 19%
Luxembourg 12%
Netherlands 18.5%
Norway 20%
Poland none
Portugal 17%
Spain 12%
Sweden 23.46%
Switzerland none
United Kingdom 15%
Yugoslavia 15%

The Insurance Debate

By far the most debated feature of car rental in both America and Europe is the collision or loss damage waiver (CDW/LDW), a "voluntary" added charge that can boost the daily cost of the car by as much as a third. Like "elective" surgery, the waiver can baffle unwary consumers who aren't sure whether they need it. Rental companies have no uniform policy on the waiver, and its advisability is often couched in threatening terms. Some of them warn motorists to pay for CDW coverage or face dire consequences in case of an accident, like immediate, full replacement cost of a damaged car. Be wary of any company that tries to put a "hold" on your credit card, because that hold may cancel out the rest of your credit up to its maximum limit. Some charge cards offer protection up to a dollar limit or the full value of the car, but that protection may be primary or secondary (if you have another policy providing coverage). In either case, you may have to pay accident bills and wait for reimbursement from your charge-card or insurance company. All of this can effectively cancel any contingency reserve that most prudent travelers bring abroad with them.

There are a few ways to make an end run around this particular hassle. For one thing, some waiver clauses began to look like a scam designed to mislead consumers, allowing rental companies to advertise low daily rates and recoup the difference with high add-on charges. Some U.S. state legislatures (New York, for example) passed laws limiting the motorist's liability for car damage to a modest fee, usually equivalent to the deductible on an insurance policy. If this counter-movement spreads, it will clearly affect the policies of large international chains and may be of some benefit to European travelers through modified liability clauses or lower waiver costs. Several major U. S. car-rental companies already include full CDW coverage, less a deductible, in their rental agreements. You may already have the coverage for rental-car damage through your regular auto policy. Be sure to read your policy carefully and check with your agent before entering into a rental agreement. We haven't accepted and paid for waivers in the continental United States, Hawaii, or Alaska for years, but our company is not licensed to write European coverage. Some U.S. auto insurers do include worldwide coverage for rental cars, and others can provide it for an additional premium; British companies write coverage for the Continent on a trip-by-trip basis. Of course, you run the risk of upping your basic auto policy rates if there is an accident, but if you rent abroad frequently or for a long period, getting your own insurance coverage will be less expensive than buying waivers.

Liability insurance is probably no different for you abroad than it is at home. European Community countries have required third-party personal injury insurance since 1974 and are now implementing a requirement for third-party property damage. If you have enough coverage on your own car in the United States, you probably have enough for car rental, but check to be sure that your coverage applies in Europe; with British insurers, you have to make special arrangements to extend coverage to the Continent. When you make such inquiries about coverage, be sure to specify the countries you intend to drive in. Before the remarkable opening of Eastern Europe in 1990, many countries were excluded from coverage—some like Albania, still are; others in Western Europe, such as Luxembourg, have rigid underwriting regulations that encourage outside companies to exclude them. It is usually cheaper to buy additional protection from your carrier at home than from a car-rental company at the daily rate. Also, your home policy liability protection is likely to be greater than a rental company is willing to provide. If you are a member of the American Association of Retired Persons (AARP) you can receive additional liability coverage by listing AARP identification numbers on the car-rental agreement. Some current numbers include: Avis AA359800, Hertz 50075, and National 6100120 (check these and bring the AARP card on trips).

To summarize: Call your insurance carrier before you leave home to find out what property and liability coverages you may already have for a European rental. Also check the fine print in your major credit card agreements for coverage, and then plot your course through the insurance maze. The situation is still volatile as we go to press: Watch it, ask questions as you shop for rental rates, and be cautious.

Car Rental in Eastern Europe

Everything is changing with amazing rapidity in Eastern Europe, and car rental is becoming easier than ever before. Some of the large U.S. companies have added more cars to their fleets there, and more franchise car-rental agencies are also opening their doors. Some companies accept payment only in easily convertible currencies, such as dollars, marks, and yen, or with a credit card. If you are driving a car that needs unleaded fuel, finding it may be a problem for some time in Eastern Europe, although the number of stations providing it is increasing rapidly. (All new cars in the European Community must be fitted with three-way catalytic converters after 1992.) Check on the necessity of buying gas and toll coupons at the border in some countries, like Italy; since these coupons reduce the high cost of fuel and motorway use significantly, it is usually wise to buy the maximum number you are allowed. (Note, however, that motorways in many countries are entirely free.)

Sources of Rental Cars

Many travel agents' computers can sort out the best rates for rentals as well as report on special charges. If you have faith in an agent's thoroughness and access to detailed European information, he or she can save you time and trouble. (But note that many American agents have only a portion of the available information on European rentals to work with, so you may wish to make some additional inquiries on your own.) Airlines offer fly-drive packages that are often very good buys, although they sometimes come with restrictions on the size of the car.

Companies specializing in European rentals include tour operators such as Kemwel and Europe by Car; they use cars from European and U.S. rental companies and sometimes offer cheaper rates. Or they may be multinationals, including large U.S. chains such as Avis, Hertz, Budget, and Thrifty. European multinationals such as Europcar and Ansa are represented in the United States by National and American International. Multinationals often give more flexible terms than smaller, country-based companies. Ask about "touring" rates when calling any company; they are often significantly cheaper for a rental period of five to seven days, or longer. For all rentals check the extras that are not included in the agreement, or you may find unexpected charges on the bill.

Car-Rental Companies

Ansa International (800) 527–0202
Auto Europe (800) 223–5555
Avis (800) 331–1804; (081) 848–8765 in U.K.
Budget (800) 472–3325; free 0800 181–181 in U.K.
Connex International (800) 333–3949; (081) 749–9110 in U.K.
DER Tours (800) 421–4343; (800) 252–0606 in California
Dollar (800) 421–6878; (800) 421–6868 in Alaska and Canada;
    (071) 935–6796 in U.K.
Europcar (800) 227–3876; (071) 834–8484 in U.K.
Europe by Car (800) 223–1516; (800) 252–9401 in California
Foremost Euro-Car (800) 423–3111; (800) 272–3299 in
    California
Hertz (800) 654–3001; (081) 679–1799 in U.K.
Kemwel (800) 678–0678
Kenning (800) 227–8990; (0246) 208–555 in U.K.
Marsans (800) 223–6114
National (800) CARRENT
Thrifty (800) 367–2277; (081) 203–7666 in U.K.
Woods of Reigate (800) 526–2915 in U.K.
World Wide Car Hire (0) 273 203366/205025 (24 hours)
    in U.K.

Special Offers from Rental Companies

Avis offers "Personally Yours" travel planning guides complete with sight-seeing information and maps. An international message center is also popular with travelers who can receive messages from friends or relatives at home as well as report itinerary changes for people who call in. The Avis "Know Before You Go" service can be activated by calling (212) 876–AVIS. Travelers can get information for most European countries on driving distances, gasoline prices, and weather, and ask other questions of Avis representatives.

Hertz maintains a computer personalized itinerary service. Travelers type a destination into the computer at the desk, and the machine will print out directions from the airport desk to your destination, including distance in kilometers and driving time. Hertz also has a translation service through AT&T using a three-way conversation with an interpreter.

Kenning Car Rental offers a "Silver Service" touring package complete with a cassette recording on driving regulations, touring, and sight-seeing. The Kenning Hotline Helpline is available twenty-four hours a day to answer questions on sight-seeing, directions, traffic rules, and other touring information.

World Wide Car Hire offers a totally inclusive package price—there are no hidden costs anywhere. Their philosophy is expressed by one word—simplicity. Tariffs include unlimited mileage, VAT/local taxes, airport surcharges, third-party insurance, and collision damage waiver. In addition there is no charge for out-of-hours delivery, baby seats, roof racks, ski racks, and snow chains. If you're going skiing at high altitudes, don't forget the snow chains!

Ask about special features offered by other companies. They sprout up quickly in a highly imitative market, but sometimes wither away when their competitive advantage disappears.

Car Rental Checklist

Many of the details of renting a car in Europe are the same as they are in the United States or elsewhere. The process becomes nearly automatic for those who do it frequently, but some extra care may avoid hitches that could mar the pleasure of a driving vacation in Europe. Consider the following:

Early Planning
- Nature of touring terrain
- Scope of proposed itinerary
- Maps of touring area and major cities within it

Choice of Vehicle
- Size of car based on number of passengers
- Suitability of car for terrain
- Standard or automatic transmission
- Trunk or hatchback (trunks hide luggage better)

Regulations and Needed Documents
- Regulations for drivers under twenty-six or over seventy
- Registration and Green Card (International Motor Insurance)
- Countries that require translation of home driver's license
- Countries that require an International Driving License

Questions to Answer Before Signing
- Drop-off charges
- Car damage and liability insurance
- Additional taxes (VAT) or service charges
- Extra charge for more than one driver
- Procedure if car breaks down
- Surcharge for filling tank at end of rental
- Service and repair facilities in touring areas
- Unlimited or limited mileage, with charges for excess mileage
- Corporate or other discounts available
- Restrictions, if any, on border or ferry crossings
- Variations in rental rates within touring area
- Variations in weekend and weekday rates for short trips
- Advantages of prepaying or guaranteeing payment with a credit card
- Additional conditions (usually in fine print on the back of the rental form)
- Accident procedure: required notifications (rental-car company, insurer, police), statements, and recording of details

- Pickup service at airport
- Arrangements for express check-in (if any) at airport drops

Checks to Make Before Driving Off
- Warning triangle provided and/or required
- Kit of spare bulbs and fuses provided and/or required
- Location of jack and spare tire
- Condition and inflation of tires
- Inspection for dents and scrapes

CAR LEASING

If you're going to be driving in Europe for a period of three weeks to three months, you may want to consider leasing a car. You'll drive a brand-new car, and the price covers all initial costs, including insurance and registration; you pay for fuel and repairs. The advantages of leasing are unlimited mileage and lower costs; they are most evident in countries with high VAT's (25 percent in Belgium and France) that are passed through to renters but not levied against nonresident purchasers. These short-term leasing arrangements, generally limited to a minimum period ranging from twenty-two to thirty-three days and a maximum of six months, do not involve the complications of long-term open or closed-end leases. They are far simpler purchase-repurchase agreements that work because they allow the leasing company to resell slightly used cars at lower tax rates or turn them into rental cars.

Because such schemes save the most money where VAT is high, there are many opportunities in Belgium and France. Cars available for lease include Audi, Volkswagen, Citroen, Peugeot, and Renault. Some leasing programs also offer lodging with the car.

Companies specializing in car leasing include: Auto Europe (800) 223–5555, Connex (800) 333–3949, Europe by Car (800) 252–9401, France Auto Vacances (212) 867–2625, Kemwel (800) 678–0678, and Renault (800) 221–1052.

CAR PURCHASE

For those lucky people who plan to drive in Europe for three months or longer, or for those who simply want to buy a European car at lower cost, it makes sense to buy a new car and bring it home. We have done this six times, picking up new Simcas, Saabs, Volvos, and Volkswagens in various European locations— and it has worked out well for us each time. In choosing to buy abroad, you save the cost of a rental car, pay less for the same car in Europe, often have it shipped home free, and have the fun of driving your own car while on vacation there. Even if you plan to be in Europe only for a matter of weeks, but want or need a new European car, it often makes sense to order abroad and use the delivery as the excuse for a touring vacation. Occasionally European car dealers in the United States will offer car pickup vacation packages when they cannot get enough deliveries to meet local demand.

The advantages of European delivery schemes hinge on various forms of tax relief that are carefully regulated. Cars purchased under diplomat and tourist sales programs *must* be exported from Europe within twelve months or become liable to extraordinarily heavy taxation or even confiscation. They cannot be sold abroad or for a fixed period of time, usually at least a year, within the country they are exported to, to prevent profiteering. Ordinarily all the tax relief is built into the initial program, but if the car will remain in a single country for more than six months, it is a good idea to check what needs to be done. In Britain, for example, you must apply to extend the tax relief or pay car tax and VAT totaling 40 percent of the value of the car.

The cost savings of buying abroad have four sources: 1. avoidance of heavy initial car taxes and VATs that apply within European countries; 2. lower import duties, because the car is used when it arrives home; 3. lower sales taxes when you register the car at home for the same reason; and 4. in many cases, free shipment home, avoiding the transportation cost built into the list price of most cars. These savings can add up to significant differences against American prices and extraordinary ones when compared to purchasing and then reselling a car abroad. Our most recent car, for example, costs the same in British pounds as in American dollars, nearly twice the price at the exchange rate when we bought it.

You can get information on European deliveries from your local dealer or one of the companies specializing in such programs; Europe Auto Brokers, Box 214-3430 AE, Nieuwegein-Utrecht, The Netherlands, (0) 3402–6–44–94; or Europe by Car, (800) 223–1516 (800–252–9401 in California).

You can also obtain comprehensive information and assistance from car manufacturers' head offices:

In the United States:
BMW, 1 BMW Plaza, Montvale, NJ 07645, (201) 573–2100
Jaguar Cars, Inc., 555 MacArthur Boulevard, Mahwah, NJ 07430-2327, (201) 818–8500
Mercedes, 1 Mercedes Drive, Montvale, NJ 07645, (201) 573–0600
Peugeot, 1 Peugeot Plaza, Box 607, Lyndhurst, NJ 07071, (201) 935–8400
Saab Scania, 1200 Northrop Road, Meriden, CT 06450, (203) 795–5671
VW, 888 West Big Beaver Road, Troy, MI 48007, (313) 362–6000
Volvo, Rockleigh, NJ 07647, (201) 768–7300

In the United Kingdom:
BMW, Ellesfield Avenue, Bracknell, Berks, RG12 4TA, (0344) 426565
Jaguar, Browns Lane, Allesley, Coventry CV5 9DR, (0203) 402121
Mercedes, Tongwell, Milton Keynes, Bucks, MK15 8BA, (0908) 668899

Peugeot, Box 46, London Road, Ryton-on-Dunsmore,
  Coventry, CV8 3DZ, (0203) 884000
Saab Scania, Saab House, Globe Park, Fieldhouse Lane,
  Marlow, Bucks SL7 1LY, (0628) 486977
VW, Yeomans Drive, Blakelands, Milton Keynes, MK14 5AN,
  (0908) 679121
Volvo, Parkway, Globe Park, Marlow, SL7 1YQ, (0628) 477977

For long-term benefits to you at home, call several of your local dealers and compare the details of the European delivery program for each car you are interested in. The dealership does not usually make much initial profit on the transaction, but it gains a new customer and can look forward to providing continuing service after you return home. And the program might make you so happy that you'll be a repeat customer for your next car, taking delivery either at home or abroad.

Automobile manufacturers differ on the amount of lead time necessary for European delivery of cars built to American specifications. If your list of options is unusual, or your choice of colors very firm, it is best to order early. Most dealers prefer to place the order two to three months in advance, but some of them can handle an order in as little as four or five weeks. The city chosen for delivery also makes a difference in lead time, with less needed for factory deliveries than pickups in other cities. There is usually no charge when the car is picked up at the factory; charges for delivery to other cities in Europe range widely and are not always based on distance alone. The cities available for pickup and dropoff for shipment home vary considerably with different manufacturers and change frequently. Since this is a crucial part of planning any tour and estimating its cost, be sure to ask for current information (not last year's) when making inquiries.

As in ordering a car at home, the buyer has the fun of selecting colors and options. What is different for Americans used to wheeling and dealing with car salesmen is the absence of a haggle factor; you'll get a fixed factory price for the total car cost and options plus delivery charges. (If you are ordering with a trade-in, you can still play the old game on the value of that.) Insurance costs are higher for a car picked up in Europe, and sometimes there is a road tax to pay. There are also a few tricks to know: If you pick up a German car within Germany, you must pay a hefty deposit for VAT (DM 500 on our last order) that will be refunded after proof that you exported the car from Germany within six months, but the whole nuisance can be avoided by picking up the same car in a nearby country. Taken as a whole, with the exception of insurance, extra charges are small potatoes compared to the money you will save on purchase price, especially for more expensive cars, and on driving in Europe without the cost of car rental or lease.

Although European delivery programs have been running smoothly for decades, there still can be hitches. We had two hassles with our last car after five easy purchases in previous rounds. Neither was serious, but both illustrate the need to be wary about details. One of them was a result of misinformation: The U.S. distributor had assured our local dealer that we could buy their very expensive insurance for just two weeks or a month on arrival and arrange our own coverage for the remaining months abroad. This would not have been worth the trouble for a trip of two weeks or a month, but we were set to stay eight months. The insurance sold to tourists by this insurer is expensive for any driver, no matter how experienced or accident free, because it is based on rates for twenty-five-year-old German males. The unfriendly insurance logic behind such high rates holds that tourists are driving much more than normal and are unfamiliar with roads, signing, and regulations, so their exposure to accidents is higher.

Knowing that all insurers did not share this logic, we had done our homework. Since our American automobile insurance company was not licensed to extend our existing coverage to Europe, we procured two quotes from other American sources specializing in policies abroad. (If you find yourself in the same situation, try American International Global, 505 Carr Road, Wilmington, DE

19809, 302–761–3100, or consider a less expensive group tourist-insurance policy written through the same company for members of AAA. Write Insurance Service Department, AAA National Headquarters, 1000 AAA Drive, Heathrow, FL 32746-5063, or call 407–444–8585.) Since we knew we were going to be spending a great deal of time in England, we also checked British insurers and found them even cheaper, but with one annoying inconvenience: Additional coverage for driving on the Continent must be written separately for each trip. (For further information, write Automobile Association Insurance Services, Ltd., Fanum House, Basingstoke, Hampshire RG21 2EA, England, or call 0–256–20123.)

We'd thought we were fully prepared. Not so. Our otherwise flawless arrival to pick up the car was marred by a demand that we pay a ridiculous amount (more than $2,000) for ten months of German insurance. The problem turned out to be a matter of German law: The registration and insurance must be written for the same time period, so shortening the insurance would cut off the special export registration. After many costly phone calls and faxes and a letter threatening to cancel our registration, which would have made us subject to 40 percent of the value of the car in British taxes, we paid the premium—but never again. If we had picked up the car in Germany with our own insurance policy in hand, we could have completed the registration ourselves in any town; alternatively, we could have driven to Germany during a short initial registration period and extended it by showing our own new insurance. But we had missed the first option, and the second was inconvenient. So we urge you to get all details of your order clarified in writing before you go, and don't believe a dealer who tells you that errors or omissions can be straightened out on arrival. European business does not operate that way.

The second, less bothersome, hassle occurred through lack of information about changes in procedure. Only on delivery did we discover that the catalytic converter had been installed, complicating our plans to drive in Eastern Europe where unleaded gasoline was not then easily available. Of course, any new car must conform to North American specifications if its ultimate destination is the United States or Canada. Formerly, the catalytic converter (which must be removed if you use leaded gas in Europe) would have been installed either by the manufacturer just before shipment from Europe or by an American dealer at home. Now some European models are designed with intricate engineering systems to improve performance with the converter and therefore must come with the converter installed. In such cases you must seek out unleaded fuel, which is much easier to find that it was even a few years ago and should be widely available after 1992. But it is still worth checking to see when your catalytic converter will be put on if you plan to drive in remote regions of Europe.

Many European manufacturers will ship your new car home free of charge. Usually you can drop it at several ports specified by the company without cost or pay a fee to turn it in at a city of your choice. The car will turn up on a dock at the designated port of entry nearest your home, where you can pick it up, normally about six to eight weeks after you have left it in Europe. Some will bring the car to your local dealer. Preparing the car for U.S. entry is done at the port of shipment, while customs clearance, freight documentation, and insurance claims are handled by a broker at the port of entry—all for a modest fee. Arrangements for our last two purchases were even better: The car was brought to our local dealer and turned over to us there. Very painless indeed.

One warning: Don't leave *anything* in the car when it is ready for shipment. Everything not firmly attached will be stolen on the dock, routinely. Radios, tape decks, and compact disc players are particularly vulnerable. During our last shipment thieves tried to break the radio-removal code but missed in four tries and succeeded only in permanently locking the tape deck instead. Be sure to check everything very carefully when you accept your car. Theft and damage is fully covered by marine insurance, paid for by the manufacturer or tourist sales organization in most cases, but settling the claims can be a nuisance. One time when we had young children and too much gear to stagger onto the plane with, we left old clothing and towels in the closets and cupboard of our camper, very cleverly hiding some of our bulky tools, camping hatchet, dishes, stainless steel utensils, and odd items deep within the soft goods. The thieves came into the camper, with muddy boots that left tracks, dumped everything onto the floor and removed every hard item, including the mounted fire extinguisher. Petty crime does pay, apparently, at least on the docks.

TIPS FOR
THE ROAD

The information in this chapter, presented in an alphabetical format, contains advice that will enable you to prepare intelligently for automobile travel in Europe. Included here as well are tips on time zones, telephoning, weather, and other travel-related matters.

Automobile Club Membership. If you are a member of AAA or a similar organization affiliated with the International Automobile Federation, you will be granted many reciprocal privileges by European national automobile associations. In Britain, for example, both the Automobile Association and the Royal Automobile Club offer a whole range of services, including basic road rescue (and for additional fees start and relay service for passengers and broken-down vehicles). The clubs also provide weather and road updates, driving regulations in Europe and touring information on routes, excursions, restaurants, and hotels. And they sell all kinds of useful insurance policies related to cars, luggage, and comprehensive trip protection.

Auto-Train Travel (Motorail Service). You can save on gasoline costs and relax instead of struggling through long drives by putting your car on a train and letting the engineer do the work. This railway ferrying is particularly useful if you're short on time and have a fixed destination in mind—getting from London to Scotland or from Calais to the Riviera or the French Alps. Some auto-trains avoid slow mountain passes by going through tunnels, others zoom for long distances through the country; in 1993 cars will be loaded onto trains for a thirty-five-minute crossing under the English Channel. Railway companies provide auto-train service, and some are connected with ferry lines. Also available, from Rail Europe, is the Eurail Drive Pass. It also provides you with the option to travel the longer distances by train and restrict your driving to the areas surrounding your various destinations. The difference, of course, is that you don't take your own car along on the train but rent one when you disembark.

Bail Bond. Most auto clubs strongly recommend that drivers invest in a bail bond for travel in Spain. In case of an accident, you can be held and greatly inconvenienced.

Documents. Carry original vehicle registration, insurance Green Card, your home driver's license and an International Driving License, but do not leave them in a parked car if you can help it, particularly overnight. It would take too much time and trouble to replace them. We forestall such problems by leaving only copies in the locked glove box and keeping the originals with our passports and other important papers.

We like to make four copies of our passports, visas, credit cards, medical cards, voter registrations, sales receipts for cameras and lenses, tickets, travel insurance policies, and any other important travel documents. Two copies of each go into separate pieces of luggage, a third into a wallet or purse, and the last one rides with the spare tire in the car. In thirty-two years of European travel we've never been ripped off, but if we ever are perhaps at least one copy will be recoverable.

Drinking and Driving. Don't. European driving laws are much stricter than those in most American states, with far lower allowable blood-alcohol levels that are vigorously enforced by random stopping. And social customs follow the same line; those who must drive to and from a party generally designate a nondrinking driver. Jails in some countries can be quite appalling.

Driver's Physical Condition. If jet lag strikes hard, you may want to recover before starting off on a long trip. You'll need full concentration for driving in strange territory, particularly during the first few days.

Emergency Phone Numbers. Reports at this writing anticipate that the twelve European Community nations will soon introduce a new emergency service phone number, but some countries will be given until 1996 to comply. The new number will be 112. (For current numbers see listing at the end of each country chapter.)

Equipment for a Trip. Check to be sure you have a warning triangle, a first-aid kit, spare bulbs, a tire jack and wheel-nut wrench, a small tool kit, and a powerful flashlight; the first three items are required by regulations in many countries, and the latter three by common sense. A fire extinguisher is recommended (required in Greece), and snow chains are mandatory in some alpine countries or regions during winter months. Yellow lenses or deflectors are required for headlights in France. (Check for any further requirements in country chapters.)

Ferries. During high season it is advisable to book international ferries well ahead of your desired sailing, unless you can tolerate long and sometimes unproductive waits for car space. Holidays can also throw a monkey wrench into plans and keep unticketed travelers waiting in line on the docks for some time. Prices vary depending upon the season of the year. The excellent ferry system in Europe, between the Continent and Britain as well as in between long peninsular countries, is worth a bit of study when planning a route. You can cut off miles of driving and enjoy a cruise at the same time. Be aware, though, that ferry line phones and representatives in the United States change frequently. Some cruise centers handle dozens of lines and some of them are dropped or added. Also some of the routes change year by year. Consult the tourist office for internal ferry information in Denmark, Finland, and Norway; Greek ferry schedules—especially for car ferries—are notoriously inconstant and sometimes irrelevant. We once waited twenty-four hours for a vagrant ferry to take us from Agios Nikolaos in Crete to Pireaus, but it did eventually arrive. The best bet is to get local information from the ferry landings. (See country chapters for listings of ferries serving countries with deep-water ports.)

Film. Handling film can be a bothersome problem in our era of tight airport security. Many people use a lead bag for film and let it go through X-ray machines. We travel with a great deal of film, more than can easily be placed in lead bags, and feel that repeated exposure to even low levels of radiation can harm the ultimate quality of the picture. (Some professional photographers do not use lead bags because they feel that any leakage will bounce rays around inside and cause more damage than the film might otherwise sustain.) Although we are happy to fly under stringent security precautions, we sometimes find the specific procedures simultaneously ineffective and overly intrusive.

For a month's trip last summer, we bought twenty rolls of slide film in a block, leaving the plastic covering intact. The security personnel at the Rome airport ripped off the plastic and proceeded to tear open each box, take out the canister and remove the film, laughing at our distress and repeating "No problema." In Helsinki and London X-ray operators forced us to let all of our film go through the machine, which we object to because the level of radiation is controlled by a rheostat and can vary from insignificant to severely damaging levels. In Amsterdam security personnel painstakingly opened our plastic container, removed boxes of exposed film that were numbered and stacked six to a bag, took off the tape, removed the canister, and looked at each film. Thirty-two rolls and twenty minutes later we were free to proceed to the boarding area. In spite of all these hassles, our film has survived without significant damage—so far.

First-Aid Kit. A kit is mandatory in many countries. (*See* Equipment for a Trip.)

Gas or Petrol. Be careful to pump the right gas into your car in self-service stations in Europe. Often diesel pumps are lined up with all of the others, and diesel fuel will quickly muck up any engine not designed for it. Usually the green marking on the pump indicates unleaded gas, but it may take locating, and some stations will not have one. If in doubt, ask. (*See* country chapters for the appropriate phrase for unleaded gas.)

Holidays. Think thrice before planning trips on European holidays, especially Christmas, the New Year, Easter, May Day, or national holidays; the worst of these is Easter. Europeans shut everything down for holidays, so when everyone else is on the road you may choose not to be. We have disregarded this advice and our better judgment again and again, and we've always regretted it. Traveling before or after holidays is far preferable to the exasperation created by overloaded roads and packed hotels and restaurants. Off-season trips are the very best, as long as it isn't so late that the things you want to see are closed.

Horns. Some cities expressly prohibit honking horns—there may be a fine for those who do. Other cities are used to drivers with a constant hand on the horn. It won't take you long to learn the local custom, but if you are in doubt, silence is golden.

International Driving License. We recommend that Americans carry an International Driving License (obtainable through AAA before you leave home), because it is required in some countries and also may be useful in case of an accident. AAA provides a list of auto clubs abroad. You can show your AAA membership card in an office abroad and receive information and some reciprocal privileges. (*See* Automobile Club Membership.)

International Labels. Throughout Europe distinguishing labels identify the country of registration for the car. These easily visible black-on-white oval labels are 6.9 inches by 4.5 inches and are stuck to a vertical surface on the back of the car. A fine can be imposed for missing labels. (*See* Appendix.)

Keys. Having only one key to a rental car can produce some stress as you try hard not to lose it. When you get out of the car, do not lock the driver's door from the inside while the rear door is open—make it a habit to lock that last door from the outside and squeeze the key in your hand to remind you where it is before you close the last door. Keep it in a safe place, preferably on your person, in case you decide to take off your jacket and lay it on the back seat.

If you have purchased the car, of course, you can have duplicate keys made and stashed in secret places in purse, wallet, or luggage. Write the identification code number of the key, and keep it with your important documents or in your wallet in case you need to have a new key made.

Light Bulbs. A spare set of bulbs for headlights, tail lights, and parking lights must be carried in some countries, including the Netherlands, Spain, and Yugoslavia. (*See* driving regulations in country chapters.)

Lights. Lighting requirements at present are among the most chaotic parts of European driving regulations. Some countries, like Norway and Sweden, require motorists to drive with low beams on in all conditions during the day; others, like Belgium, Germany, and Yugoslavia, require them if there is reduced visibility during daylight. Many countries, including Austria, France, Germany, Greece, the Netherlands, and Switzerland, prohibit driving with parking lights only; while Italy, Portugal, and Spain prohibit driving with full headlights in built-up areas. Austria and Luxembourg require parking lights for night parking on streets without lights. Whatever logic persists throughout this maze can be attributed to the order of nature and the kind of light each country spread between the Arctic Circle and the Mediterranean receives, but it is confusing for motorists. You may want to review the requirements whenever you cross a border.

Maps. Good maps are far more essential to happy driving in Europe than in America, and far easier to obtain. A European passion for cartography has produced excellent series like French Michelins, German Halwegs, and British Ordnance Surveys in a whole range of scales for purposes as various as regional touring, mountaineering, or rambling on footpaths. If you can get to a really good map store before departure to buy the country, region, and city maps you will need for your tour, go for it. The paucity of such stores in the United States may mean waiting until arrival in Europe, but it really is better to wait than to put up with the frustration of inadequate maps. For planning purposes only, the AAA European and regional (defined as several countries) maps are very good, as long as you remember that the driving times are somewhat conservative.

Medications. If you are going to be in Europe for a long time, order any regular medications in double prescriptions (two separate bottles) with a few more pills than you think you will need in each bottle; customs officials will not question this safety strategy. Then give one set to your traveling companion, or place the second set in your luggage. When we load up pills for a long stay, we also take along a note from our doctor stating the medical purpose of the prescriptions.

Metric System. Since the world metric movement has waned or at least paused during the last decade, using this remarkably logical system can be confusing at first for American and British travelers. A rough, quick conversion may become second nature with practice. Multiply kilometers by six, and move the decimal point one place to the left to get miles. A kilogram, as in vegetables in the market, is 2.2 pounds. One liter equals 2.11 pints, 1.06 quarts, and 0.26 gallons in American measure. When buying British petrol, however, figure five Imperial gallons to six U.S. gallons. When measuring fabric 2.54 centimeters equal one inch and 1 meter equals 3.28 feet or 1.09 yards. Grams, as in airmail letters, figure 28 to the ounce. To convert Celsius or centigrade temperature to Fahrenheit, double the figure, deduct 10 percent and add 32. (*See* the Appendix for Weights and Measures.)

Packing. Packing your car can seem like a jigsaw puzzle. It helps to have everything stowed into a container, preferably a soft bag that will conform to the hole left for it. When leaving the car for sight-seeing, try to get *everything* into the trunk so as not to tempt thieves. (Station wagons are problematic on this score; think twice before renting or leasing them if you are going to spend much time in cities notorious for car theft, like Naples or Seville.) That isn't to say that thieves won't be able to whisk into the trunk, but at least you'll keep them guessing about whether it's worth the trouble.

Parking. Parking regulations vary from country to country and city to city, presenting a true maze for tourists seeking a street spot. Permissive and prohibitive markings are usually in a code of broken or solid single or double lines; for the uninitiated, a good guess is that the more markings you see the less likely it is that you will be able to park. Most marking systems are backed up by signs. Often all available street parking in cities is reserved for residents with stickers. Sometimes you need to purchase a ticket from a nearby metering machine and place it inside your window so the time can be seen from outside. Other places require a cardboard clock or disk (from a local shop or your hotel concierge) to be set and placed inside the windshield. If you disobey city parking regulations, your car may be clamped out of action with a "Denver boot." We noticed them every day in Regent's Park in London—ugly yellow metal clamps that were expensive and time-consuming to have removed. This is perhaps the least pleasant of all parking experiences in the world, best avoided by heading for the nearest garage, no matter how expensive, until you figure out how to work the system. Even in garages be sure to read all the signs carefully or you may not be able to get out without special coins or tokens after normal working hours. (*See* individual countries for more specific regulations.)

Right-of-Way. Please check the regulations listed for each country very carefully, but in general right-of-way, or priority, is given to the car coming from the right, even in Britain. (*See also* Traffic Circles/Roundabouts.)

Purchases. Keep an envelope for sales slips of purchased items that will need to be declared when you go through customs in your home country. It is much easier to keep track as you go along than to try to reconstruct purchases later, and you may be required to back up your customs declaration with receipts.

Road Signs. International road signs are standard throughout Europe, apart from some supplementary signs for each country. The uniform system is logical, complete, and graphic, rather than linguistic. The shape of the signs indicates the category of information or command. Triangular signs warn of danger, such as level railway crossings, intersections, and slick roads. Circular signs indicate restrictions or prohibitions, including no-passing zones, road closures, and one-way streets. Rectangular signs give information about important matters such as first-aid stations, telephones, garages, parking areas, and pedestrian crosswalks. (*See* the Appendix.)

Route Planning. See samples in the Introduction.

Seat Belts. Seat belts are mandatory almost everywhere for front-seat occupants and often required in the back seat when fitted. Children must also wear seat belts and may not sit in the front seat in most countries if they are under a specified age, usually ten or twelve.

Speeds. Speeds on Germany's autobahns can begin at 130 kph (about 80 mph). You may not notice someone approaching in your rearview mirror until you see his lights impatiently blinking you out of the path of the juggernaut. Much as we have always thought of the British in terms of courtesy and a propensity to queue, we've discovered that early middle-aged, and sometimes younger, drivers are usually hell-bent on getting around everyone on the highway. It doesn't pay to drive in the fast lane, as they want to roar past between 80 and 120 mph sometimes. Legal motorway speed limits in European countries range from 110 to 130 kph (68 to 81 mph), with lower limits in Denmark and Norway; other road speeds in the country vary more widely from 70 to 100 kph (43 to 62 mph), depending upon the quality of the road in some cases; and everywhere in built-up or congested areas, speeds are limited to 50 or 60 kph (31 or 37 mph).

Telephone Codes. When dialing from another country, it is important to remember to omit the "O" at the beginning of the regional or city code. We have included it in the complete code, in each country chapter, for those who are dialing within the country.

Telephone Tips. before making an international call, check the time-zone difference. Find out about surcharges (sometimes excessive) if you are calling from a hotel. Compare the costs of credit-card, collect, and station-to-station calls before you start. Americans can usually save money by connecting with the AT&T operator in the States for transatlantic calls, using special codes provided for the connection from each country; these calls are charged at cheaper rates than other transatlantic calls. It is almost always cheaper to phone from a public phone in a railway station, airport, or post office than from a hotel. When you are dressed in a bathrobe, however, you may not feel impelled to rush out to the nearest public phone; then you can place a quick call and ask to be called back for the real conversation. In rural areas where the telephone system is less sophisticated, particularly in southern Italy, Yugoslavia, Greece, and Turkey, be prepared for almost endless frustration in placing normally simple international calls.

For domestic calls, you can purchase very convenient phone cards for use in some systems, saving you the nuisance of collecting pocketloads of heavy change. Sometimes you'll need a token to make a call. When making a domestic call, listen for the dial tone, dial the code, and in some areas wait for the second dial tone before continuing with the number. As a general rule, dial carefully with no long pauses.

Time Zones. Britain, Ireland, and Portugal operate on Greenwich Mean Time, five hours ahead of U.S. Eastern Standard Time. Western Europe, including Austria, Belgium, Czechoslovakia, Denmark, France, Germany, Hungary, Italy, the Netherlands, Norway, Spain, much of Sweden, and Yugoslavia, operates on Central European Time, one hour ahead of Greenwich Mean Time. Eastern Europe, as well as Finland, Greece, Turkey, and western Russia, is two hours ahead of Greenwich Mean Time. Daylight savings time begins in the spring and returns to standard time in the fall. (Note: Daylight savings time is not changed on the same date in all countries—you'll have to ask.) The twenty-four hour military clock is generally used for all timetables and many other civilian schedules.

Tire Chains. Chains may be legally required and practically necessary in mountainous areas during the winter. Sometimes they can be purchased in towns near difficult roads, but if you know you are heading for alpine areas it makes sense to equip yourselves in advance.

Traffic Circles/Roundabouts. Traffic circles are much more frequent in Europe than in America—particularly in England, where roundabouts can interrupt traffic flow every few miles. As at any point of congestion, you must be aware of who has right-of-way. In many countries traffic entering the circle has priority over traffic already in it, but in others traffic in the circle has right-of-way, unless there are road markings indicating priority for vehicles entering from a through route. We specify these details within each country chapter, but it can be very confusing as you wonder if you should follow old instincts when in a tight situation or heavy traffic. It is helpful to get a mind-set going for each country, then concentrate on the procedure before you get to a traffic circle.

Trams. Passengers getting off a tram have absolute priority over vehicles in most European cities. Since trams (or streetcars) are rarities in American cities, many tourists may be unfamiliar with their special lanes and privileges over other traffic. Don't be surprised if they cross your path or fill your lane without any signal: They have the right-of-way.

Unleaded Gas or Petrol. Unleaded pumps are increasingly appearing all over Europe. Usually identified by a green handle, these pumps carry 95 octane in most cases. Some service stations have only one unleaded pump, others none; check carefully before you fill the tank of a car with a catalytic converter installed.

Visa. No country in this guide currently requires U.S. visitors to carry a visa. Other countries still have the requirement.

Warning Triangles. In many countries if you have an accident or a breakdown, you must place a red warning triangle 150 feet behind the car. (See country chapters for this requirement.)

Weather Conditions. Fog can be a special hazard in some areas of Western Europe, and it is particularly dangerous on motorways, where it has caused fatal pileups at excessive European speeds. Travelers caught in sudden fog need to slow down gradually (sudden braking exacerbates the danger of a pileup), keep a safe distance from the vehicle in front, use windshield wipers and low-beam headlights, and find the nearest way off high-speed roads to safer secondary roads. If you are caught in deep fog on a motorway, as we once were on the Po Valley autostrada, you can sometimes navigate by the tail lights of the vehicle ahead, but it is wise to leave by the first exit. Snow and ice call for extreme caution, reduced speed, gentle braking and steering, and use of plowed roads whenever possible, just as they would anywhere else in the world.

PART II:

COUNTRIES OF EUROPE

World renowned Lipizzaner stallions graze on the hills of Koeflach, in Austria's mountainous region. (Austrian National Tourist Office)

AUSTRIA

CAPITAL: Vienna (Wien)

POPULATION: 7,555,000

AREA: 32,701 square mi/83,849 square km

CURRENCY UNIT: Austrian schilling (AS) and groschen

LANGUAGE: German

TIME FROM UNITED STATES: Eastern Standard plus 6 hours

TELEPHONE ACCESS CODES: To United States, 00 (from Linz) or 900 (from Vienna), or USA Direct 022–903–011; from United States, 43

EMBASSIES: *American Embassy,* Boltzmanngasse 16, A-1091 Vienna, Austria; phone: 0222–31–55–11. *British Embassy,* Juaresgasse 12, A-1030 Vienna; phone: 756117/8

CONTACTS FOR PRETRIP PLANNING

Automobile Clubs

Vienna: Osterreichischer Automobil-Motorrad-Und Touring Club (OAMTC), Wien No., Burgenland, 1010 Wien, Schubertring 1-3; phone: (0222) 71199–0 or (for road service) (0222) 711–997. *Linz:* 4024 Linz, Wankmullerhofstrasse 58; phone: (07222) 41–3–71. *Salzburg:* 5020 Salzburg, Alpenstrasse 102-104; phone: (622) 20–5–01. *Innsbruck:* 6020 Innsbruck, Andechsstrasse 81; phone: (512) 44–5–21

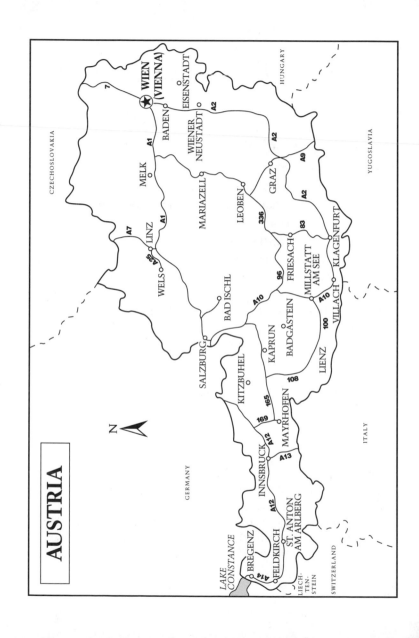

Tourist Offices

United States: Austrian National Tourist Office, 500 Fifth Avenue, New York, NY 10110; phone: (212) 944–6880. *Britain:* Austrian National Tourist Office, 30 St. George Street, London W1R 0AL; phone: (071) 629–0461

Austria: Vienna Tourist Board, Palais Grassalkovics, A-1025 Vienna, Austria; phone: (011) 43–1–211140. Salzburg City Tourist Office, Auerspergstrasse 7, A-5024 Salzburg, Austria; phone: (011) 43–662–80720. Innsbruck City Tourist Office, Burggraben 3, A-6020 Innsbruck, Austria; phone: (011) 43–512–59850

Airlines

Austrian Airlines: *United States,* (800) 843–0002; *Britain,* (071) 439–0741

TOPOGRAPHY

Austria's three alpine chains are separated by valleys providing easy access to mountain terrain even during the winter. We have chosen to ski in Austria a number of times and have skimmed along the valleys to the point where our route headed upward— that's the time to put on chains.

It is relatively easy to drive around within one of Europe's most mountainous countries and to reach its six neighbors by road, because the valleys separating the country's three alpine chains contain major roadbeds stretching along the lengthy east-west axis of the country. Consequently, an almost uninterrupted motorway links Vienna to Salzburg, Innsbruck, and Switzerland. Another almost-completed motorway heads southwest from Vienna to Graz and Italy.

Crossing these long arteries are three north-south motorways:

The short western one connects Innsbruck with northern Italy; the longer middle one links Salzburg with Germany in one direction and Italy in the other; and the eastern one runs all the way from Linz to Yugoslavia. The missing links, not needed much until recently, are in flat land from Vienna southeastward toward Budapest and northwestward toward Prague. On these routes anticipate slow driving with heavy truck traffic and long lines at border crossings.

Motorways include: the Westautobahn from Salzburg to Vienna, Inntal from Kufstein to Innsbruck, Brennerautobahn from Innsbruck to the Brenner, and sections between Bregenz-Feldkirch-Bludenz. Salzburg–the Lueg Pass–Spittal an der Drau; Klagenfurt–Villach–Arnoldstein; Vienna–Wiener Neustadt–Grimmenstein; Vienna–Schwechat Airport; Traboch–Graz–Strass; and Graz–Wolfsberg.

In a country blockaded by mountains on three sides and strung out along a central spine of high alps, two dozen passes and tunnels are crucial. Many of the major ones—Arlberg, Brenner, Felbertauern—are kept open throughout the winter, but others, like the Grossglockner, are open only during the summer and early fall. Those who choose to explore the more remote mountain roads and passes in the summer will find driving the minor highways slow but unforgettable. Hikers and climbers heading for the great blank spots on the map can drive to the edges of them, but the secondary roads leading into the high mountains should be treated with great caution in bad weather.

ROAD CONDITIONS

Highways are well maintained and open in winter, except for some mountain passes that are closed. Information on passes:

Achen: 990 meters in height, Route 307 Tegernsee to Jenbach; open in winter

Annaberg: 976 meters, Route 20 St. Pölten to Mariazell; usually open in winter

Arlberg: 1,793 meters, Route 190 Feldkirch to Innsbruck; usually open in winter

Brenner: 1,380 meters, Route 182/12 Innsbruck to Bolzano; usually open in winter, chains sometimes necessary

Felbertauern Tunnel: 1,605 meters, Route 108 Mittersill to Lienz; open in winter

Fern: 1,209 meters, Route 314 Imst to Reutte or Nassereith to Telfs; sometimes closed in winter

Flexen: 1,773 meters, Route 198 Stuben to Lech/Arlberg; sometimes closed in winter

Gerlos Platte: 1,629 meters, Route 165 Zell am Ziller to Mittersill; recommend using the toll road, as the old road is steep and in bad condition; usually open in winter

Grossglockner: 2,505 meters, Route 107 Bruck to Lienz, tunnel at summit; closed November–May

Hochtannberg: Route 200 Egg to Warth; open May–October

Katschberg: 1,641 meters, Route 99 Spittal to St. Michael; usually open in winter

Loibl: 1,067 meters, Route 91/1 Klagenfurt to Ljubljana; open June–November

Plocken: 1,360 meters, Route 110/52B Kötschach-Mauthen to Tolmezzo; open April–November

Potschen: 982 meters, Route 145 Bad Ischl to Bad Aussee; usually open

Pyhrn: 945 meters, Route 138 Windischgarsten to Liezen; usually open

Radstadter-Tauern: 1,738 meters, Route 99/(E14) Radstadt to St. Michael; use toll road and tunnel; usually open in winter

Reisa: 1,510 meters, Route 315/40 Landeck to Malles; usually open

Semmering: 985 meters, Route 17 Gloggnitz to Mürzzuschlag; usually open in winter

Silvretta: 2,032 meters, Route 188 Schruns to Ischgl; closed November–May

Thurn: 1,273 meters, Route 161 Kitzbühel to Mittersill; usually open

Timmelsjoch: 2,474 meters, Route 186/446 Otz to Merano; closed October–May

Turracher HoHe: 1,763 meters, Route 95 Predlitz to Feldkirchen; usually open in winter

Wurzen: 1,072 meters, Route 83/1A Villach to Kranjskagora; closed October–May

HIGHWAY SIGNS

The road system includes motorways *(autobahnen)*, expressways *(schnellstrassen)*, federal highways *(bundesstrassen)*, provincial roads *(landesstrassen)*, and communal roads *(gemeindestrassen)*.

White letters and numbers on a green background indicate European highways. White numbers on blue background are for the Austrian Federal highways (type 1) on which right-of-way is given to all intersecting traffic. Yellow circular signs with black numbers indicate Austrian Federal highways (type 2) where there is no special right-of-way.

DRIVING REGULATIONS

• Minimum driving age here is eighteen years of age. Non-residents must carry a driver's license from home. In addition, an

International Driving License is strongly recommended. Car registration papers are required.

• Insurance policies need to have minimum coverage of $695,000 for any damage or injury caused. Austrian law stipulates that the person who causes damage or injury is liable for the balance remaining unpaid after the insurance settlement to the unlimited extent of his or her personal property.

• General speed limits are 50 kph/31 mph in town, 100 kph/62 mph on roads and highways out of town, and 130 kph/81 mph on expressways.

• The driver and front-seat passenger must wear seat belts. Children under the age of twelve years are not allowed to ride in the front seat, but infants may ride there when placed in a rear-facing baby seat.

• Vehicles must carry a warning triangle and first-aid kit.

• Driving is on the right, passing on the left. Traffic approaching from the right has right-of-way.

• On mountain roads vehicles moving uphill have right-of-way.

• Dimmed headlights must be used when meeting other vehicles.

An area in which custom differs: flashing headlights are not a friendly "go ahead" but a warning, "watch out, here I come."

PARKING

Blue Zones in towns are indicated by NO PARKING signs with the words ZONE or KURZPARKZONE. Motorists must buy parking tickets from banks, tobacconists, or machines in the parking area. In some places a parking disk placed inside the windshield is used to indicate the time car was left.

Parking is prohibited within 15 meters of pedestrian crossings and of public transportation stops. Most other prohibited places are familiar to all drivers, such as entrances to houses, buildings, and service stations.

EMERGENCY INFORMATION

After an accident motorists may call 133 for police, 122 for fire, or 144 for ambulance. Be sure to use the local prefix number.

GASOLINE STATIONS

Gasoline stations are located frequently in populated areas. Before driving in the mountains it is wise to fill up your tank; it doesn't cost any more to run on the top half. Unleaded gasoline is *bleifrei.*

BELGIUM

CAPITAL: Brussels (Bruxelles)
POPULATION: 10,000,000
AREA: 11,915 square mi/30,550 square km
CURRENCY UNIT: Belgian franc (BF)
LANGUAGES: Flemish, Dutch, German, and French
TIME FROM UNITED STATES: Eastern Standard plus 6 hours
TELEPHONE: access codes: to United States, 001 or USA Direct
  11–0010, from United States, 32
EMBASSIES: *American Embassy:* 27 Boulevard du Regent, B-1000
  Brussels; phone: (02) 513–3830. *British Embassy:* Brittania
  House, rue Joseph II 28, 1040 Brussels; phone: (02) 217–9000

CONTACTS FOR PRETRIP PLANNING

Automobile Clubs

Brussels: Touring Club de Belgie (TCB), Wetstraat 44, 1040
  Brussels; phone: (02) 233–2211. Koninklijke Automobielclub
  van Belgie VZW, Aarlenstraat 53 1040 Brussels; phone: (02)
  230–2211

Tourist Offices

United States: Belgian National Tourist Office, 745 Fifth Avenue,
  New York, NY 10150; phone: (212) 758–8130. *Britain:* BNTO,
  Premier House, 2 Gayton Road, Harrow, Middlesex, HA1 2XU,
  England; phone: (081) 861–3300. *Belgium:* 61 Rue Marché aux
  Herbes, 1000 Brussels; phone: (02) 512–3030

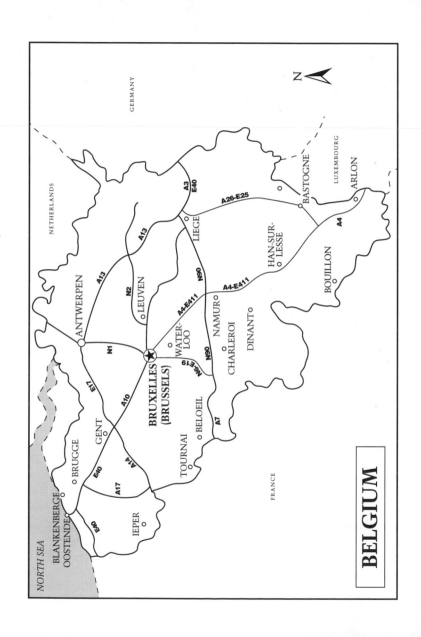

Ferries

P and O European ferries: *United States,* through International Cruise Center, (800) 221–3254; *Britain,* Dover (0304) 203388 and London (081) 575–8555; *Belgium,* Car Ferry Terminal, 8380 Zeebrugge, phone: (050) 542222; or Régie voor Maritiem Transport, 5 Natienkaai, B-8400 Ostend, phone: (059) 707601. Routes from Ostend and Zeebrugge to Dover

North Sea Ferries: *United States,* (800) 221–3254; *Britain,* (0482) 77177 for reservations and 795141 for general inquiries. Routes from Kingston-upon-Hull to Zeebrugge

Travelers should carefully check off-season rates and schedules, which are not as frequent as those in high season.

Airlines

Sabena World Airlines: *United States,* (800) 541–4551 or (516) 466–6100; *Britain,* (081) 780–1444

TOPOGRAPHY

Belgium's topography can be divided into three broad sections: a large central plain, coastal lowlands along the North Sea in Flanders, and the Ardennes plateau rising in the southeast. Each has its characteristic terrain, and all are quickly reached through one of Europe's most complete motorway networks.

In the province of Brabant, at the heart of the central plain surrounding Brussels and Waterloo, the land is quite flat and the density of roads unusually high. Brussels is the major hub not only of Belgium but of a large portion of Western Europe as well, and all major roads lead to or skirt around it. Yet a carefully planned radial system reduces "crossroads" congestion and makes it easy to reach a circle of interesting destinations nearby, including Antwerp, Louvain, and Ghent. At the northeastern fringe of the central plain, in the provinces of Antwerp and Limburg,

The Castle of the Counts of Flanders, in Ghent, stands as a reminder that the city was a center of mercantile power for centuries. (Belgian National Tourist Board)

road density thins out a bit in a terrain of rolling dunes and marsh-land.

To the west in Flanders, Belgium's 46 miles of sandy coast is loaded with beach resorts all linked together by a single major road that is not all limited access expressway, unfortunately. The major roads will zip you through Flanders in no time, but you won't catch the changing character of the landscape—rolling hills and river valleys, all interlaced with a network of canals—unless you poke along the secondary roads. And in some cities where canals are primary, like Bruges, you'll be better off abandoning your car and moving around via canal boats and footbridges.

South and east of the central plain, the land begins to rise into the foothills of the Ardennes. Here again the routes dictated by motorway engineering will speed you through the country without letting you appreciate its deep river valleys. To do so you must leave the high-speed roads radiating from Brussels and drive the shore roads along the Meuse or other rivers. In the higher forested sections of the Ardennes, narrow steep valleys with winding roads are equally attractive, but slow.

The Brussels ring road is actually two ring roads, inner and outer, and both are outside of the old town. The inner ring takes drivers through many tunnels. Because the traffic moves fast, it is helpful to be familiar with the names of major roads near your desired exit. Road numbers are not always given.

ROAD CONDITIONS

In general the major roads in Belgium are in good condition and well maintained. Some are quite new, including the Brussels–Luxembourg Expressway completed in 1989. The driving time between the two cities is now two hours instead of three. The system is elevated, and additional access ramps have been added. It is well lighted, as are all of Belgium's major roads. (A friend told us that a woman driving alone at night consequently can fccl completely confident.) Another new freeway was recently completed between Liège and Luxembourg.

The following roads link Belgium with all of its neighbors:

E40: Ostend, Bruges, Ghent, Brussels, Liège, Aachen
E19: Rotterdam, Antwerp, Brussels, Waterloo, Nivelle (E10 joins) (A2 joins) (A1 and E15 join), Paris
E42: Dunkerque, Lille, Mons, Liège (A40 joins), Aachen

The last time we picked up a new car in Europe, it was in Brussels. We couldn't have had an easier entrée as the new car became familiar to us. Belgium has lots of straight, wide, safe roads—no tricky little narrow streets winding up steep hills without proper street signs. Not that you can't drive those too—we can and we did. But it's nice to begin life in a new car with ease. Streets in Brussels are well marked, and the traffic isn't anything like the madness one encounters in some other large cities. Motoring is rarely restricted by weather conditions. During storms the Ardennes area may require care on snow and ice. A greater danger is fog, which has caused serious pileups on major roads.

HIGHWAY SIGNS

Belgium's toll-free motorways have two different numbering systems. "A" roads signify a national system using black-and-white signs. "E" roads are part of a newer international system of green-and-white signs. "N" roads have a fairly new numbering system and may contain two numbers, both the old and the new. Signs in the south of Belgium are in French; in the north in Dutch.

DRIVING REGULATIONS

• The rule of the road is to drive on the right, pass on the left. At junctions right-of-way is given to traffic approaching from the right. On roundabouts yield to the traffic entering the circle.

• Motorists must carry a National or International Driving License as well as vehicle registration.

• Insurance is compulsory. Travelers are advised to carry the international "Green Card."

• Safety belts must be worn in town and on the highway, by all persons, front and back.

• Children under twelve years of age may not sit in the front seat if places are available in the rear.

• Unless indicated by a signal, the speed limit in built-up areas is 60 kph/37 mph. Outside built-up areas the speed limit is 120 kph/75 mph on motorways and roads with at least four lanes; 90 kph/55 mph on all other roads.

• Bicycles have the right-of-way when they are continuing ahead past an intersection. Motorists should be aware of a painted line along the cycle track found on one or both sides of some roads. Do not turn if a cyclist is approaching.

• Headlights must be on low beam at night.

PARKING

It is useful to carry coins of 5 francs and 20 francs for parking. Some cities and towns have metered parking, others require parking dials set inside the windshield. There are parking garages in large cities and towns.

Some hotels have their own parking spaces, but others depend upon municipal garages. *Always be aware of opening and closing hours* of parking garages on weekends and holidays. We once neglected to read signs on the wall as we parked our car.

The next morning, when rushing to get on the road in time to make the ferry in Ostend, we could not get the car out. After reading the signs we found that a combination of coins would release the barrier.

You cannot see much of the cities or towns from a car. Find a parking space and move about the older sections of town on foot. In large cities the car will be useful when visiting sites outside of the old town.

In Brussels visitors will not want to drive in the restaurant area from late afternoon through the evening, because people walk in the narrow streets as they check the menus.

EMERGENCY INFORMATION

In case of accident the police should be notified by calling 101 (or 106 in Antwerp, Bruges, Brussels, Charleroi, Ghent, or Mechelen). Call 100 for Ambulance or Fire. Warning triangles must be carried in case of a breakdown. They are to be placed behind the vehicle at a distance of 30 meters on most roads and 100 meters on motorways. They must be large enough to be visible at 50 meters.

GASOLINE STATIONS

You'll encounter stations frequently. There is no problem when leaving the airport or dealership. Some stations close at 8:00 P.M. and reopen at 8:00 A.M., but stations on motorways and main roads are open twenty-four hours, including Sundays. Unleaded gasoline is marked *essence sans plomb loodvrije benzine.*

CZECHOSLOVAKIA

CAPITAL: Prague (Praha)

POPULATION: 15,000,000

AREA: 49,920 square mi/128,000 square km

CURRENCY UNIT: koruna (KCS)

LANGUAGES: Czech (Bohemia and Moravia), Slovak (Slovakia)

TIME FROM UNITED STATES: Eastern Standard plus 6 hours

TELEPHONE ACCESS CODES: to United States, 001 or USA Direct 00–420–00101; from United States, 42

EMBASSIES: *American Embassy,* Trziste 15, 12548 Prague; phone: 53–6641/8. *British Embassy,* Thunovska Ulice, 14 Mala Strana, 11800 Prague; phone: 533–3407 or –3408 or –3409. *United States:* Czechoslovakian Embassy, 3900 Linnean Avenue NW, Washington, D.C. 20008; phone: (202) 363–6315. *Britain:* Czechoslovakian Embassy, 28 Kensington Palace Gardens, London W8 4QY; phone: (071) 727–3966 or CEDOK Ltd., 17-18 Old Bond Street, London W1X 4RB; phone: (071) 629–6058

CONTACTS FOR PRETRIP PLANNING

Automobile Clubs

Prague: Ustredni Automotoklub CSSR, Opletalova, 29 116 31, Prague 1; phone: 223544–7 or 224906/773455 or 223592

Tourist Offices

United States: CEDOK, 10 E. Fortieth Street, New York, NY 10016; phone: (212) 689–9720. *Britain:* CEDOK, 17/18 Old Bond Street, London W1X 3DA, England; phone: (071)

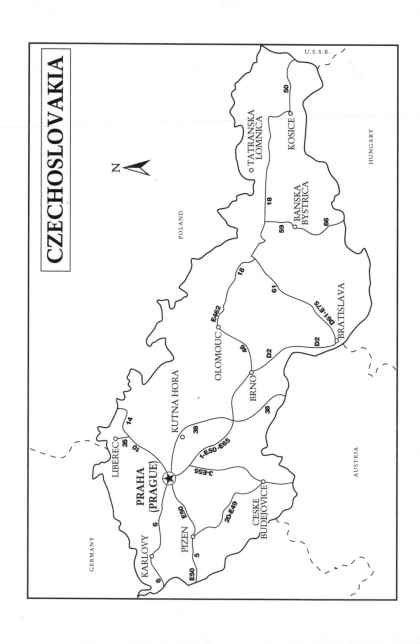

629–6058/9. *Czechoslovakia:* CEDOK, Na Prikope 18, Prague 1; phone: (42) 2–2127–111

Airlines

Czechoslovak Airlines: *United States,* (800) 223–2365 (New York), (800) 628–6107 (Chicago); *Britain,* (071) 255–1366 or 1898

TOPOGRAPHY

From a driver's point of view, there are two important things to remember about the topography of Czechoslovakia. First, mountain ranges stand on four of its five borders (Austria is the exception), and that makes getting in and out slow but interesting. Second, as you drive from west to east inside the country, the plateau of Bohemia merges into the hills of Moravia and finally the mountains of Slovakia, part of the high Carpathian ranges that dominate Eurasia. The largest cities of the three regions— Prague, Brno, and Bratislava—are joined by Czechoslovakia's only completed motorway. Apart from a few motorway spurs, other cities and tourist destinations are reached by a rather thin but well-maintained network of two-lane highways.

The road system is most developed in Bohemia, on the western side of the country. There is a surprising variety of topography at destinations within half a day's drive from Prague— famous spas in the region between Carlsbad (Karlovy Vary) and Pilsen (Plzen) to the west, mountain terrain for hiking and skiing in the Krkonose National Park to the north, and a lake district to the south. The upper stretches of Bohemia's rivers, which flow all the way to the North Sea, have cut narrow gorges well worth driving if you have the time to wind along beautifully paved cartroads. The same may be said of Bohemia's magnificently situated castles, which look so close on the map; never underestimate how long it might take you to reach them.

As the land becomes generally hilly and then mountainous in Moravia and Slovakia, the river valleys become more important as lines of communication than as scenic drives. Here, on the other side of the divide, rivers flowing into the Danube provide roadbeds for the major highways, most of them on a northeast-southwest axis. They link cities like Brno and Bratislava to the hiking country of northern Moravia and the high peaks of the national parks in the Tatra region of Slovakia. The latter is Czechoslovakia's prime alpine resort area, where major road coverage (apart from one curiously placed stretch of motorway) is not yet fully developed.

ROAD CONDITIONS

The main roads are in good condition, with reflectors on posts along the side. The motorway from Bratislava to Brno to Prague is smooth and fast, but some of the little country roads can be twisty and slow. Most main roads bypass villages. Mountain roads deserve some caution, as in other parts of Europe.

Hard shoulders are notably lacking, even on some main highways. In rural areas most main roads carry foot and horse-drawn traffic as well as high-speed vehicles, so drivers need to watch out for sudden stops and rapid slowdowns.

HIGHWAY SIGNS

Road signs follow the Convention on Road Signs and Signals (Vienna, 1968).

It will be useful to know the translation of the following signs: *Prujezd Zakazar:* closed to all vehicles. *Jednosmerny Provoz:* one-way traffic. *Dalkovy Provoz:* bypass. *Objizdka:* detour. *H Nemocnice:* hospital. *Chodte Vlevo:* pedestrians must walk on the left.

DRIVING REGULATIONS

• The speed limit is 60 kph/37 mph in built-up areas from 5 A.M.–11 P.M. At night the speed limit is the same as outside built-up areas: 110 kph/68 mph on motorways and 90 kph/56 mph on other roads.

• The speed limit at level crossings is 30 kph/19 mph for 30 meters before the crossing.

• Drive on the right and pass on the left. Vehicles coming from the right have right-of-way at road intersections not marked by a sign.

• Drivers and front-seat passengers must wear seat belts, if the car is fitted.

Zamek Hlvboka is but one of many castles dotting the landscape of Czechoslovakia. (CEDOK, Czech Tourist Board)

- Children under the age of twelve are not allowed in the front seat.
- A warning triangle is required, as well as a first-aid kit and spare vehicle light bulbs.
- Any visible damage to a car entering Czechoslovakia must be certified by authorities at the border. If any damage occurs inside the country, a report must be obtained at the scene of the accident. Damaged vehicles may be taken out of the country only after this evidence is produced.
- Drivers must be eighteen years old to drive.
- An International Driving License is required.

PARKING

Vehicles must park on the right side of the road. On one-way streets parking is also allowed on the left.

Drivers must not park where visibility is poor or where the vehicle would cause an obstruction, including within 5 meters of an intersection, pedestrian crossing, a bus or tram stop, or within 15 meters of a level crossing.

EMERGENCY INFORMATION

The emergency number for Autotourist is 154, police 158, ambulance 155, and fire department 150.

GASOLINE STATIONS

Visitors may buy nonrefundable gasoline coupons for a 20 percent reduction from CEDOK, banks, and at the borders.

Stations on international roads and in major towns are open twenty-four hours a day. Unleaded gas is labeled *beg olova, olovinatych prisad, natural 91.*

DENMARK

CAPITAL: Copenhagen (Kobenhavn)

POPULATION: 5,119,200

AREA: 16,799 square mi/43,075 square km

CURRENCY UNIT: Danish krone (DKR)

LANGUAGE: Danish

TIME FROM UNITED STATES: Eastern Standard plus 6 hours

TELEPHONE ACCESS CODES: to United States, 009 or USA Direct 0430–0010; from United States, 45

EMBASSIES: *American Embassy,* Dag Hammarskjolds Alie 24, 2100 Copenhagen O; phone: (01) 42–31–44. *British Embassy,* 36–38–40 Kastelsvcg, DK-2100 Copenhagen; phone: (01) 26–46–00

CONTACTS FOR PRETRIP PLANNING

Automobile Clubs

Copenhagen: Forenede Danske Motorejere (FDM), Blegdamsvej 124, DK-2100 Copenhagen; phone: (31) 38–21–12. *Aalborg:* FDM, Vesterbro 65, DK-9000, Aalborg; phone: (98) 12–11–44. *Aarhus:* FDM, Storetorv 6, DK-8000, Aarhus C; phone: (106) 13–13–44. Odense:FDM, Vindegade 26-28, DK-5000, *Odense:* C; phone: (66) 13–34–80

Tourist Offices

United States: The Danish Tourist Board, 655 Third Avenue, Eighteenth floor, New York, NY 10017; phone: (212) 929–2333. *Britain:* Danish Tourist Board, Sceptre House, 169-173 Regent

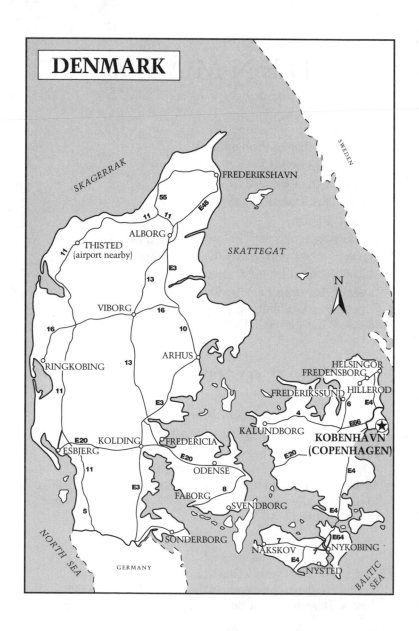

Street, London W1R 8PY; phone: (071) 734–2637/8.
Denmark: Danish Tourist Board, H. C. Andersens Boulevard,
Copenhagen; phone: 22–33–11–13–25

Ferries

Color Lines: *United States,* c/o Bergen Line (800) 323–7436 or
(212) 986–2711; *Britain,* (0473) 23–30–44 or 23–05–30 or (091)
257–9682. Routes from Hirtshals to Newcastle, Kristiansand,
and Oslo

Scandinavian Seaways Ferry Lines: *United States,* EuroCruises
(800) 688–EURO; DFDS Travel Center (800) 533–3755 or (305)
491–7909; *Britain,* (0255) 240240. Routes from Esbjerg to Harwich or Newcastle, Copenhagen to Oslo

Airlines

SAS: *United States,* (800) 221–2350; Britain, (071) 734–4020

TOPOGRAPHY

Looking at a road map does not convince one that Denmark
hangs together topographically, but it does. One part is the Jutland peninsula attached to the continent, and the other consists of
482 islands (not counting the remote Faroes), only about a hundred of which are inhabited.

Touring Jutland is relatively straightforward. A motorway runs
from the German border as far north as Aarhus, and a pervasive
network of primary and secondary roads extends throughout the
rural areas of the peninsula. That network makes it easy to reach
a variegated landscape—flat marshes in the south, sand dunes
and barrier beaches along the North Sea in the west, a pocket of
lakes concentrated around Silkeborg in the center, narrow fjords
indenting the northeast coast, and broad ones in the northwest.

The rest of Denmark consists of three major archipelagoes and one isolated island separated from Jutland and each other by sea channels called "belts." Only the narrowest of these, between Jutland and Funen, is bridged. The car ferry from Funen to Lolland takes 45 minutes, and the main route across the "Great Belt" from Funen to Sealand takes an hour. (This last crossing, in the middle of the partially completed motorway linking Odense with Jutland and Copenhagen, may eventually be replaced by a tunnel.) Those driving up from the south can choose to ferry across these belts to reach Sealand and Copenhagen, or they may cross from Germany by ferry to the southern islands of Lolland and Falster, where completed motorways lead to Copenhagen. Ferry connections to various points across the channel in Sweden are quick and easy from Elsinore (25 minutes) or Copenhagen (an hour to an hour and a half). Reaching Bornholm, Denmark's easternmost island beyond the tip of Sweden in the Baltic, is another matter: It takes about seven hours by car ferry from Copenhagen.

If all this sounds terribly complicated, it isn't in practice. Denmark's internal and external car ferries are frequent and efficient, and usually need to be reserved in advance only during peak travel times in the summer and around holidays (though it's always wise to check booking policy on long external ferries). And once ashore on the major islands, you will find efficient road networks almost everywhere. This is particularly true on Sealand, where motorways extend northward and westward from Copenhagen, and a series of rings encircle the city. If you have the time, it is almost always rewarding to take smaller roads through the countryside or along the coast, particularly to interesting sections like the "Danish Riviera," between Copenhagen and Elsinore.

ROAD CONDITIONS

Roads in Denmark are in good condition and well maintained. Some new sections of motorways have been built, especially the E47 and E20 in Sealand, the E45 on Jutland, and the E20 from west to east on Fyn. Of course, much of the travel in Denmark is by ferry, and the Danish Tourist Office can provide a ferry guide. Weather rarely restricts driving in Denmark.

HIGHWAY SIGNS

International road signs are used throughout Denmark. Translations of the following signs will be useful: *Ensrettet korsel:* one-way street; *Fare:* danger; *Farligt sving:* dangerous bend; *Gennemkorsel forbudt:* no through road; *Hold til hojre:* keep to the right; *Hold til venstre:* keep to the left; *Indkorsel forbudt:* no entry; *Korsveg:* crossroads; *Omkorsel:* detour; *Parkering forbudt:* no parking; *Vejarbejde:* road torn up; *Vejen er spaerret:* road closed.

DRIVING REGULATIONS

• Drive on the right, pass on the left. When approaching an intersection without signs, the driver on the right has right-of-way. On traffic circles the driver must yield to the traffic from the left.
• If a series of triangles called "shark's teeth" are pointing toward you, you must yield.
• Dimmed lights must be used.
• Seat belts must be worn by drivers and front-seat passengers.
• A warning triangle is required.
• Speed limits on motorways are 100 kph/62 mph; on other roads outside built-up areas 80 kph/50 mph, and in built-up areas 50 kph/31 mph.
• Pedestrians have the right-of-way at pedestrian crossings.

PARKING

Parking disks are required where there are no parking meters in Copenhagen. Disks are available from FDM offices, tourist offices, service stations, banks, and post offices.

Agri Bavnehoj, the highest point (450 feet) in the Mols Hills of East Jutland, commands a wide view of land and seascape. (Danish Tourist Board/John Sommer)

EMERGENCY INFORMATION

In an emergency call the police, fire department, or ambulance by dialing 000.

GASOLINE STATIONS

Gasoline stations are located all over Denmark. There are increasingly more twenty-four-hour stations that contain self-service pumps. Unleaded gasoline is called *blyfri benzin.*

Salisbury Cathedral soars over a rural landscape, presenting a striking contrast between nature's tranquility and man's achievement. (West County Tourist Board)

ENGLAND AND WALES

CAPITAL: London

POPULATION: 46,221,000

AREA: 27,742 square mi/71,131 square km

CURRENCY UNIT: British pound

LANGUAGE: English

TIME FROM UNITED STATES: Eastern Standard plus 5 hours

TELEPHONE ACCESS CODES: to United States, 010 or USA Direct 800–89–0011; from United States, 44

EMBASSIES: *American Embassy,* 24/31 Grosvenor Square, W., London 1A1AE; phone: (071) 499–9000

CONTACTS FOR PRETRIP PLANNING

Automobile Clubs

Basingstoke: The Automobile Association, Fanum House, Basingstoke, Hants RG21 2EA; phone: Basingstoke 20123. *London:* Royal Automobile Club, 49 Pall Mall, London SW1Y 5JG; phone: (071) 839–7050. *East Grinstead:* The Caravan Club, East Grinstead House, East Grinstead, West Sussex, RH19 1UA; phone: (0342) 327410

Tourist Offices

United States: British Tourist Authority, 40 W. Fifty-Seventh Street, New York, NY 10019; phone: (212) 581–4700; *England:* British Travel Centre, 12 Regent Street, London SW1; phone: (071) 730–3400

Ferries

Bergen Line: *United States,* (800) 323–7436 or (212) 986–2711

B & I: *Britain,* (071) 734–4681 or 7512 or (051) 227–3131; routes from Holyhead to Dublin; Pembroke Dock to Rosslare

Brittany: *United States,* (800) 221–3254 or (516) 747–8880; *Britain,* Portsmouth (0705) 827701 and Plymouth (0752) 221–321; routes from Portsmouth to Caen and St. Malo, Plymouth to Roscoff and Santander

Color Line (once Norway Line and Jahre Line, now merged): *United States,* c/o Bergen Line (800) 323–7436 or (212) 986–2711; *Britain,* (091) 296–1313; routes from Newcastle to Bergen and Stavanger, Amsterdam to Bergen and Stavanger, and Kiel to Oslo

Hoverspeed: *United States,* (212) 599–5400; *Britain,* (0304) 240241; routes from Dover to Calais and Boulogne, Portsmouth to Cherbourg

North Sea: *United States,* (800) 221–3254; *Britain,* (0482) 77177 for reservations and (0482) 795141 general inquiries; routes from Hull to Zeebrugge and Rotterdam

Olau Ferry Line: *Britain,* (0795) 666666; routes from Sheerness to Vlissingen

P and O European Ferries: *United States,* (800) 221–3254 or (516) 747–8880; *Britain,* Dover (0304) 203388, London (081) 575–8555; routes from Dover to Zeebrugge, Ostend, Calais, Boulogne, Felixstowe to Zeebrugge, and Portsmouth to Le Havre and Cherbourg

Sally Line: *Britain,* (0843) 595522; route from Ramsgate to Dunkerque

Scandinavian Seaways: *United States,* EuroCruises (800) 688–EURO; DFDS Travel Center (800) 533–3755 or (305) 491–7909; Britain,(0255) 240240; routes from Harwich and Newcastle to Esbjerg, Gothenburg, and Hamburg

Sealink Stena Line: *Britain,* (0233) 647047; routes from Folke-
stone to Boulogne, New Haven to Dieppe, Southampton to
Cherbourg, Fishguard to Rosslare, Holyhead to Dun
Laoghaire, Stranraer to Larne, Portsmouth to Fishbourne and
Ryde on the Isle of Wight, and Lymington to Yarmouth on the
Isle of Wight

Airlines

British Airways: *United States,* (800) 247–9297; *Britain,* (081)
897–4000; Virgin Atlantic: *United States,* (800) 862–8621

TOPOGRAPHY

Those used to vast spaces separating touring destinations—especially Americans and Australians—will be pleasantly surprised by
the compression of England and Wales. Driving distances from
London measure just about 300 miles to the outermost edges—
Land's End in Cornwall, Holyhead in Wales, or the Scottish border. But the road system serving this compact country has almost
as much variability as the terrain itself, ranging from one-lane
roads (with passing zones) to winding country lanes, secondary
roads, primary highways, dual carriageways, and motorways.

Since Britain came late into the superhighway age, its network
of motorways is relatively sparse. The first, opened in 1960, heads
north from London to Leeds, and now a branch skirts Birming-
ham and Manchester on the way to the Lake District and the
Scottish border. Shorter motorways spread out from London to
Dover, Cambridge, Oxford, Bristol, Exeter, and Southampton.
Apart from a few cross-links in the midlands, that is the extent of
the system to date. The staple for the rest of the primary road system is dual carriageway (divided four-lane highway with unlimited access), a relatively efficient compromise apart from the
handling of highway junctions. At some point British highway en-
gineers got married to the concept of roundabouts (circles or ro-

taries), and the result is an endless progeny of traffic interruptions on most major routes, especially in densely populated areas.

Secondary roads (and some primary ones, too) dive right into an unspoiled countryside preserved by the "green belt" concept that decreed, some forty years ago, that towns must end at a sharp boundary and be surrounded by a wide swath of open land. Thus you will see through your car windows something hardly imaginable in many other countries—pure landscape undesecrated by suburban sprawl, factories, roadhouses, or billboards.

The rolling downs (hills) of southeastern England (Kent and West and East Sussex) are very pleasant to drive through, but be prepared to crawl through villages and roundabouts with long lines of traffic, graphically called "tailbacks," during busy periods. There is no network of fast roads in an east-west direction. Like spokes of a wheel, a few main arteries radiate out from London to the coast, but they are not always fast, either. Sections of two motorways do extend toward Canterbury and Brighton, and a new one to Folkstone will eventually connect with the Eurotunnel.

Several dual carriageways lead to the south and southwest; but, except on the motorway from London to Southampton, driving in Hampshire, Wiltshire, and Dorset can be very slow and frustrating. A motorway heads due west from London to Bristol and Southern Wales, with a spur southwest to Exeter. Devon and Cornwall have a special charm for drivers who like meandering down isolated single-lane roads that tunnel between hedgerows— lovely to look at and sometimes exciting, because one never knows what is coming around totally obscured curves.

The center of England is heavily populated, with the growth of London reaching out to new towns in an expanded urban area. Yet the counties around the periphery of London provide some of the best car touring in England, like the Norfolk roads to the east and the Cotswolds to the west. Driving in the congestion of Greater London is another matter. Moving anywhere inside the "orbital" (London's fancifully named outer ring road) is problematic at any time other than late evenings or Sunday mornings.

With one exception, there are no motorways leading into, much less through, the heart of London's two centers, the West End and the City.

Consequently, if you're inclined not to try driving in London, you may be wise, but we have managed for thirty years by picking up a few tricks from the ubiquitous London cabbies. The first rule is never to use the orbital during peak rush hours, and the second is to remember that many alternative routes do exist to cross the city a bit faster, in almost any direction; but you should plan them in advance or you will be confused by too much information on the frequent signs along such routes.

Farther north in the midlands, the rolling land has been scarred by heavy industrialization, and motorists will find much road construction with all of its annoying delays. Yet in the midst of large cities, between Manchester and Sheffield, lies a hiker's refuge from overpopulation, the empty moors of Derbyshire's Peak District. To the northwest lie the gems that make driving in Britain so rewarding—the Yorkshire moors and dales, the Lake District, and the mountains of Snowdonia in Wales.

ROAD CONDITIONS

As we mentioned in the Introduction, driving in England has changed since we first visited forty years ago. In those days everything was slow and winding, with fewer cars on the road. Now the small roads are still the same, with hedgerows you can't see over in some areas, but the charm of the place makes slow going worthwhile. But clogged motorways are the bane of anyone going anywhere, especially on a holiday weekend. Much as we love England and keep going back, we have to be realistic about driving on motorways. The M25 around London is by far the very worst; built as the answer to congestion, it was outdated before it was finished. Cars are backed up during all rush hours and whenever construction is in progress. Motorists who live outside of London have the choice of taking the M25 part of the way or winding through towns with many roundabouts (traffic circles) and congestion.

Before leaving on a lengthy Easter visit to Scotland, we plotted possible courses heading north on a map with English friends. We knew all of the advantages and disadvantages of each motorway. Heading north long before the holiday began was not bad, but coming home at the end was sheer madness. Long lines of cars stretched for miles, inching along if not stopped totally. We finally decided to get off and try to make progress on country roads in a zigzag course as we yearned for our flat in London. Nine hours later we finally oozed into town. We still traveled every long weekend researching this book and others for almost five months, but chose our departure time and roads very carefully.

In conclusion we recommend driving for pleasure all over England when others are not also on the road. If you can travel off-season you can breeze along; at other times you know you will be among other vacationers.

HIGHWAY SIGNS

Motorways are classified "M" and compare with U.S. interstate highways. Those marked with "M" in parentheses will eventually be motorways. Primary roads are marked "A" and are like U.S. multilanes, with a number of them divided highways. Other roads are marked "B."

DRIVING REGULATIONS

• Visitors planning to drive in Great Britain are always apprehensive about driving on the left, but that doesn't turn out to be a problem. We have usually driven a left-hand–drive car, which can be a little harder if driving alone, because you can't see around lorries (trucks) to pass. In a right-hand–drive standard-transmission car, the other hand seems able to shift on the "wrong" side. Of course we have wondered if old instincts would snap into place in case of a tight situation. This just serves to heighten driving awareness, however, which isn't a bad idea.

• Drivers must drive on the left and pass on the right, after checking the mirror and signaling.

• Sometimes as we drive off the ferry in Dover, we have to remember the rules for roundabouts, which are doubly confusing compared to our usual patterns in the United States. The rule is that when entering a circle, you must yield to any traffic on your right unless road markings at the edge of the roundabout indicate that you have right-of-way. Remember that you are going around toward the left. In case there are two lanes heading into the roundabout: If you are going to take the first turnoff, then stay in the left lane; if you are continuing around the roundabout, stay in the right lane, and move over in advance of your turnoff. Use your left signal to indicate that you are turning left immediately; or the right signal, if you are continuing around, until you have passed the exit before the one to be taken, at which point you will switch on the left signal.

• The speed on motorways and dual carriageways (two lanes each way) is 70 mph, other roads 60 mph and in built-up areas 30 mph.

• Seat-belt use is compulsory.

• Pedestrians have the right-of-way when they are on the black-and-white zebra crossings. You must not pass in the area marked by zigzag lines on the approach to a zebra crossing. At pelican crossings (crossings operated by pedestrians who push a button to change stop and go signals for motorists) the signals have the same meaning as traffic lights, except that a flashing amber signal will follow the red stop signal. When the amber light is flashing, you must yield to any pedestrians on the crossing.

PARKING

Drivers may not park within the area marked by zigzag lines on either side of a zebra crossing nor in the zone indicated by rows of studs on the approach to pelican crossings.

Parking disks or parking tickets obtained from a machine in the parking area are necessary along most streets and in parking lots.

EMERGENCY INFORMATION

The national emergency telephone number, 999, connects you with police, fire brigade, and medical service. The Automobile Club emergency number is (081) 954–7373.

GASOLINE STATIONS

Petrol stations are everywhere in England. Many of them now sell unleaded petrol (gas) at green pumps, marked "unleaded BS7070 premium."

Warwick Castle, completely intact, overlooks the River Avon.
(Warwick Castle)

Savonlinna, a city in the heart of the Finnish Lake District, provides access to Europe's largest inland-waterway system. (Finnish Tourist Board)

FINLAND

CAPITAL: Helsinki

POPULATION: 4,918,000

AREA: 131,906 square mi/338,221 square km

CURRENCY UNIT: Finnish markka (FIM)

LANGUAGES: Finnish and Swedish

TIME FROM UNITED STATES: Eastern Standard plus 7 hours

TELEPHONE ACCESS CODES: to United States, 990 or USA Direct 9800–100–10; from United States, 358

EMBASSIES: *American Embassy,* Itainen Puistotie 14A, Helsinki; phone: 171931. *British Embassy,* 16-20 Uudenmaan Katu 00120, Helsinki 12; phone: 647922

CONTACTS FOR PRETRIP PLANNING

Automobile Clubs

Helsinki: Autolitto, Auto and Touring Club of Finland, Kansa Koulukatu 10, 00100 Helsinki 10 SF; phone: 694–0022. Finnish Travel Association, Mikonkatu 25, Helsinki 10; phone: 80–170868

Tourist Offices

United States: Finnish Tourist Board, 655 Third Avenue, New York, NY 10017; phone: (212) 949–2333. *Britain:* Finnish Tourist Board, 66 Haymarket, London SW1Y ARF; phone: (071) 839–4048. *Finland:* Tourist Information, Unioninkatu 26, SF-00130 Helsinki; phone: (9) 0–144–511, postal address: Finnish Tourist Board, PB 53, SF-00521 Helsinki

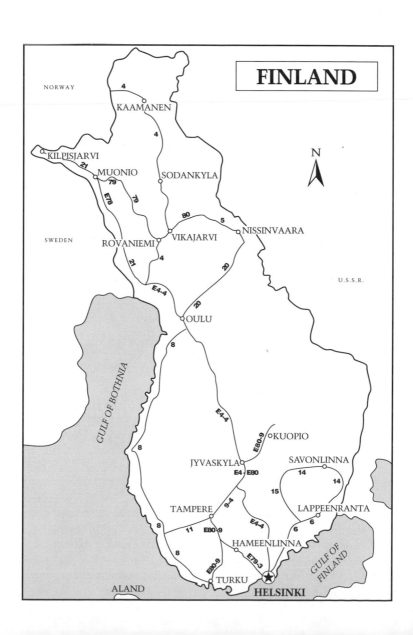

FINLAND

NORWAY

KAAMANEN

4

4

KILPISJARVI

21

MUONIO

79

SODANKYLA

E78

79

SWEDEN

80

5

ROVANIEMI

VIKAJARVI

NISSINVAARA

U.S.S.R.

21

4

20

E4-4

20

OULU

8

N

GULF OF BOTHNIA

E4-4

E80-9

KUOPIO

JYVASKYLA

SAVONLINNA

E4 E80

14

14

15

8

9-4

E4-4

LAPPEENRANTA

TAMPERE

11

E80-9

6

8

HAMEENLINNA

6

E80-9

E79-3

GULF OF FINLAND

ALAND

TURKU

★ HELSINKI

Ferries

Silja Line: *United States,* (800) 323–7436 or (212) 986–2711;
Viking Line: *United States,* EuroCruises (800) 688–EURO;
   Finland, 09–12351

Airlines

Finnair: *United States,* (800) 950–5000 or (212) 689–9300;
   Britain, (071) 408–1222

TOPOGRAPHY

Finland has no accessible borders for those driving from the
south and west. Luckily, it has the largest, newest, and most luxu-
riously appointed car ferries in Europe to make reaching Finland
by sea a pleasant part of anyone's journey. Two competing lines,
Silja and Viking, provide service to and from Sweden, Germany,
Poland, and Estonia, as well as St. Petersburg to the east.

Finland's geography and topography (65% forest, 10% inland
water) result in a population spread very thinly everywhere except in the south coastal region. This statistic tells a tale for
drivers because the road system, though good, is appropriate for
the density of population. So don't expect an abundance of motorways leading into the forest or the arctic tundra.

The south coastal region from the Russian border to major
cities like Helsinki and Turku provides the most normal driving
situation. Although there are few motorways, most of them
around Helsinki and Turku, they are extended through much of
the southern belt by improved, limited-access highways called
"motortrafficways." Just north of this coastal belt, Finland's huge
and magnificent lake district begins, occupying somewhere between a quarter and a third of the country as a whole. Here you
may be tempted to park for a day or a week and take to the lake
steamers, particularly on routes with names like the "Silver Line"

or "Poet's Way." Yet an intricate network of paved primary and secondary roads makes most of the district accessible by car.

A totally different watery region begins as you move westward along the south coast from Helsinki toward Turku and beyond: solid land gradually disintegrates into thousands of islands, forming one of the world's most beautiful archipelagos. This is more a domain for cruising sailors than touring drivers, but you can enjoy it on a car ferry to Aland (and Stockholm, if you are headed for Sweden).

As you drive northward toward the Arctic Circle and Lapland, roads and population become sparser. Beyond Rovaniemi, situated just south of the Circle, there are only two major roads to Lapland, one leading northwest to Sweden and the other due north to Norway's arctic coast. Drivers here should watch both the weather and the level of their fuel tanks and be prepared for sections of gravel road. But you can anticipate what's coming: Each year the tourist authority distributes an up-to-date map of summer roadworks all over the country that is particularly useful to drivers heading for more remote regions with fewer alternative roads.

ROAD CONDITIONS

Finnish roads are maintained in good condition. All main roads are kept open all winter, including those in the north (some of these may be rough during spring thaw). Snow tires are recommended in some areas.

HIGHWAY SIGNS

International signs are used in Finland. All public roads are numbered as follows: 1st-class main roads: 1–39; 2nd-class main roads: 40–99; important highways: 100–999; other: 1,000–2,999; local roads: 11,000–19,999. Numbers M1 to M999 are motorways.

It could be useful to know the following translations: *Kokeile jarruja:* test your brakes. *Aja hitaasti:* drive slowly. *Tie rakenteilla:* road under construction. *Paallystetyota:* resurfacing road. *Kunnossapitotyo:* road repairs. *Ajo sallittu omalla vastuulla:* driving permitted at your risk. *Varo irtokivia:* beware of loose stones. *Aluerajoitus:* local speed limit. *Kelirikko:* Frost damage.

DRIVING REGULATIONS

• Drive on the right, and pass on the left. At intersections drivers on the right have right-of-way except when encountering a main highway.

• There is a variable speed limit of 60-80-100 kph/37-50-62 mph, and restrictions are listed on signs. If no signs are posted, the basic speed limit is 80 kph/50 mph. On motorways the speed limit is 100 kph/62 mph. The usual speed limit in built-up areas is 50 kph/30 mph.

• Every visitor must have a driver's license and a decal on the car showing the country of origin. The green card, not required, is useful in case of an accident.

• All occupants must wear seat belts whether riding in front or in back of the car.

• Dimmed headlights are compulsory outside of built-up areas, even during the day. They may also be used in built-up areas.

• Horns must not be used in towns and villages, except in an emergency.

PARKING

Parking regulations follow international practice. Parking meters are standard in Helsinki, and they are checked frequently.

EMERGENCY INFORMATION

In an emergency dial 000.

GASOLINE STATIONS

Stations are available in most of Finland, but less often in the far north. At self-service stations prices are lower. Unleaded gasoline is marked *lyijyton polttoaine.*

FRANCE

CAPITAL: Paris
POPULATION: 53,400,000
AREA: 208,099 square mi/533,587 square km
CURRENCY UNIT: French franc (FF)
LANGUAGE: French
TIME FROM UNITED STATES: Eastern Standard plus 6 hours
TELEPHONE ACCESS CODES: to United States, 19 or USA Direct
19–0011; from United States, 33
EMBASSIES: *American Embassy,* Avenue Gabriel, 75008 Paris;
phone: 42–96–12–02 or 42–61–80–75. *British Embassy,* 35, rue
du Faubourg St.-Honoré, 75383 Paris; phone: 42–66–91–42

CONTACTS FOR PRETRIP PLANNING

Automobile Clubs

Paris: Automobile Club de France, 6-8 place de la Concorde, F-
75008 Paris; phone: 42–65–34–70 (International Service Number: 42–27–82–00. Association Française des Automobilistes, 9,
rue Anatole-de-la-Forge, 75017 Paris; phone: 42–27–82–00

Tourist Offices

United States: French Government Tourist Office, 610 Fifth
Avenue, New York, NY 10020; phone: (212) 757–1125 or
(900) 420–2003. *Britain:* French Government Tourist Office,
178 Piccadilly, London, WIV OAL; phone: (071) 499–6911
(recording) or 491–7622. *France:* Maison de la France, 8,
Avenue de l'Opéra, 75001 Paris; phone: (1) 42–96–10–23;
toll-free assistance hotline in France: 05–20–12–02

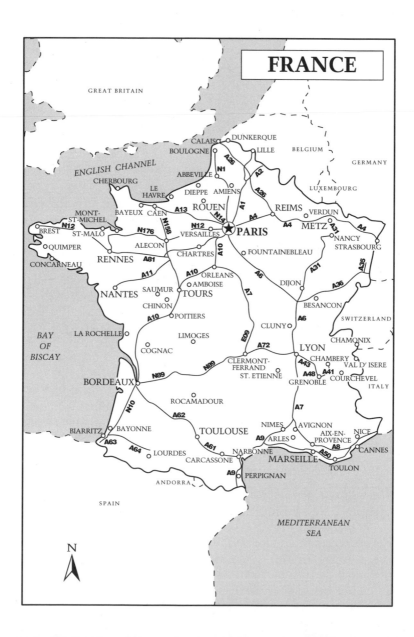

Ferries

Brittany Ferries: *United States,* c/o International Cruise Center, (800) 221–3254 or (516) 747–8880; *Britain,* Portsmouth (0705) 827701 and Plymouth (0752) 221–321. Routes from Caen and St. Malo to Portsmouth; Roscoff to Plymouth

Hoverspeed: *United States,* (212) 599–5400; Britain, (0304) 240241. Routes from Calais and Boulogne to Dover; Cherbourg to Portsmouth

P & O Ferries: *United States,* (800) 221–3254 or (516) 747–8880; *Britain,* Dover (0304) 203388, London (081) 575–8555. Routes from Calais and Boulogne to Dover; Le Havre and Cherbourg to Portsmouth

Sally Line: *Britain,* (0843) 595522

Sealink Stena Line: *Britain,* (0233) 647047. Routes from Boulogne to Folkestone; Dieppe to New Haven; Cherbourg to Southampton

Airlines

Air France: *United States,* (800) 237–2747; Britain, (071) 499–9511

TOPOGRAPHY

Exploring France by car has special pleasures and few driving problems. The country's topographical variety is a marvel of perfect completeness, rivaling in small scale terrain that spreads out over whole continents in North America or Australia. We can't think of anything that's missing—perfect sandy beaches, rocky coastlines, a warm Mediterranean riviera, fertile plains, quiet river valleys, near-desert plateaus, and mountains of all varieties. And you can reach it all quickly and easily, logging hundreds rather than thousands of miles on your odometer.

A highly efficient and comprehensive road system makes all this possible. Autoroutes provide very fast transit from region to region. Most radiate from Paris, but there are subsidiary networks in the regions around the English Channel, the French Alps, and the Riviera, as well as a great circle enclosing almost the whole southern half of the country. When you reach the region of your choice, you will probably want to leave the autoroutes and main highways for more scenic secondary roads.

In the northeast, the topography ranges from agricultural plain to vineyard slopes and the massive folds of the Jura ridges. Routes across the Jura Mountains from Besancon toward Geneva are slow, but the views are worth it—in good weather. Once we struggled through this route during a winter afternoon and evening of fog and rain and vowed never to do that again.

In the north and west, one encounters both the battleground and playground of northern France, but the best parts of the northern region are beyond the reach of the autoroutes to Rouen and Caen. The fine-sand beaches of Normandy, where Allied Forces stormed ashore in 1944, are now quiet resort areas backed by rolling hills covered with orchards. Farther south, the tidal island of Mont St. Michel marks the northern end of the almost extravagantly picturesque drive along the Brittany coast. Farther south and east, the Loire Valley is more quickly reached by the autoroute from Paris to Tours, leading to fairyland chateaus and a string of superb vineyards.

The southwestern regions—Aquitaine, Midi-Pyrenees, Roussillon, and Languedoc—are encircled by autoroutes on their periphery, but you must use smaller roads to get into their quite distinctive landscapes. The pastoral Dordogne Valley is in small scale, with prehistoric caves and overhanging limestone cliffs best seen from byroads. Farther south, space expands in the dryer, more austere landscape around Toulouse and Carcassonne. To the north lie the high plateaus and mountains of the Massif Central, and to the south the high peaks of the Pyrenees along the Spanish border, a favorite destination for trout fishing, mountain hiking, skiing, and exploring Basque villages.

In the southeast—Provence, Cote d'Azur, the Riviera, Savoie and the Mont Blanc region—drivers encounter extremes of terrain, but autoroute networks lead directly to the sea or the mountains. Provence has the Maritime Alps, chalk cliffs, and the Camargue or floodplain of the Rhone; for all but the latter, you must leave the valley highways and drive minor roads to see the best of the landscape. The Cote d'Azur and Riviera from Marseilles to Monaco is a stretch of dramatic Mediterranean coast dotted with fine beaches and international resorts, all of which can be seen from the twisting corniche drive carved into the cliffside. Farther north, the high alps of Dauphine and Savoie—extending eastward from Grenoble and Mont Blanc into Italy and Switzerland—are France's prime center for mountain climbing and high-altitude skiing. As such, the region is well served by fast roads in the lower valleys, many of them developed for the Winter Olympics sites in Grenoble and Albertville. But driving the narrow, winding roads into the upper valleys can be a slow process, and it often requires chains in the winter.

In the center of it all is Ile de France, with all spokes leading to Paris—hub of art, architecture, business, fashion, politics, and savoir vivre as well as highways. The city is surrounded by grand parks, palaces, and cathedrals—Chantilly, Fontainebleau, Versailles, and Chartres—which are easily reached by car through the system of autoroutes radiating from the outer and inner ring roads. But, and it is a big *but,* driving the inner ring road, called the "Peripherique," can be just as exciting as anything you will do in the city, especially during rush hours. There is very little advance notice of exit lanes and highway splits, and even less tolerance for lane switches by speeding Parisians. Inside the Peripherique, traffic jams are frequent and lengthy. If you are going to spend much time in the city, we suggest parking your car and leaving it until you next want to visit a place outside the rings.

ROAD CONDITIONS

France maintains an excellent, carefully graded road system, with many autoroutes spanning the entire country. Some of it was designed during the Napoleonic era, with much expansion since.

Information on mountain passes:

Allos: 2,250 meters in height, Route D908 Barcelonnette to Entrevaux, closed early November–mid-June

Aravis: 1,498 meters, Route N509 Annecy to Chamonix, closed late November–late March

Aspin: 1,489 meters, Route N618 Arreau to Luz St.-Sauveur, closed mid-December–late March

Aubisque: 1,710 meters, Route N618 Laruns to Argeles-Gazost, closed late November–mid-June

Ballon d'Alsace: 1,178 meters, Route D465 St.-Maurice-sur-Moselle to Belfort, intermittent closure December–April

Bayard: 1,246 meters, Route N85 Grenoble to Grasse (Route des Alpes), intermittent closure

Cayolle: 2,356 meters, Route D902 Barcelonnette to Nice, closed November–May

Chat: 637 meters, Route N514a Yenne to Le Bourget-du-Lac, open in winter

Col de Braus: 1,002 meters, Route D2204 Nice to Col de Tende, usually open

Col de Brouis: 879 meters, Route D2204 Nice to Col de Tende N204, open in winter

Col de Montets: 1,461 meters, Route N506 Chamonix to Martigny, closed November–late May

Col de Tende: 1,321 meters, Route N201 La Giandola to Borgo S. Dalmazzo S20 Tunnel at summit, intermittent closure

Croix de Fer: 2,067 meters, Route N526 La Mure to St.-Jean-de-Maurienne, closed November–May

Croix Haute: 1,179 meters, Route N75 Grenoble to Sisteron, open all year

Faucille: 1,320 meters, Route N5 Morez to Geneva, intermittent closure

Built in the twelfth century and partially collapsed since the seventeenth, the Pont St. Benezet once spanned the Rhone. (French Tourist Office)

Galibier: 2,556 meters, Route N202 St.-Michael de Maurienne to Lautaret Saddle, closed mid-October–late June

Iseran: 2,770 meters, Route N202 Lanslebourg to Bourg St.-Maurice, closed late October–early July

Izoard: 2,360 meters, Route D202 Briançon to Guillestre, closed late October–early July

Larche: 1,996 meters, Route 21 Cuneo to Barcelonnette, intermittent closure

Lautaret: 2,058 meters, Route N91 Briançon to Vizille, intermittent closure

Mt. Genèvre: 1,854 meters, Route N94/24 Briançon to Turin, usually open; chains needed in winter

Petit St.-Bernard: 2,188 meters, Route N90 Bourg St.-Maurice to Aosta, closed late October–mid-June

Peyresourde: 1,563 meters, Route D618 Arreau to Bagnères de Luchon, intermittent closure

Port: 1,249 meters, Route D618 St.-Girons to Tarascon-s-Ariège, intermittent closure

Pourtalet: 1,794 meters, Route N134/C136 Pau to Huesca, closed November–late May

Puymorens: 1,915 meters, Route N20 Toulouse to Bourg Madame, intermittent closure

Quillan: 1,714 meters, Route N118 Carcassonne to Mont Louis, intermittent closure

Restefond: 2,678 meters, Route D64 Jausiers to St.-Etienne de Tinee, closed October–early July

Somport: 1,631 meters, Bedous to Jaca, intermittent closure

Tourmalet: 2,115 meters, Route N618 Luz St.-Sauveur to Arreau, closed mid-November–late June

Vars: 2,109 meters, Route D902 Barcelonnette to Guillestre, closed December–March

Mont-St.-Michel, an abbey and refuge dating back to the eighth century, rises from tidal flats that once isolated it. (French Tourist Office)

HIGHWAY SIGNS

Routes nationales are national roads exhibiting N before the number. *Routes départementales,* or provincial roads, are indicated by a D. Some of the old N roads are now D roads, keeping their old numbers preceded by a 9. *Itineraires de délestage* are roads that avoid cities. Blue signs with yellow arrows signal the motorist to these roads. Green arrows on white signs are roads leading from Paris; green-and-white arrows on a white background are found on roads leading to Paris. Autoroute signs conform to international signs.

DRIVING REGULATIONS

• Drive on the right, pass on the left. Drivers must yield to vehicles on a major road. At the intersection of two roads and at traffic circles drivers must give way to traffic on the right.

• Drivers must carry a valid driver's license from their country of residence.

• The international Green Card is compulsory, and the insurance must be valid for the entire trip.

• Speed limits are 130 kph/81 mph on toll autoroutes, 110 kph/68 mph on dual carriageways (four-lane roads) and autoroutes without tolls, 90 kph/55 mph on other roads and 60 kph/37 mph in towns. If the roads are wet, the limits are 110 kph/68 mph on toll autoroutes, 100 kph/62 mph on dual carriageways and nontoll motorways, and 80 kph/50 mph on other roads. The word *rappel* means a continuation of the restriction. There is a new minimum speed limit of 80 kph/50 mph for the outside lane on autoroutes during daylight, on level ground, and with good visibility.

• It is compulsory for the driver and front-seat passenger to wear seat belts.

PARKING

Parking disks must be used in cities with a blue zone. Some places have automatic machines, located along a street or in a parking lot, where tickcts may be bought and placed inside the windshield. Gray zones have parking meters. On dark streets parking lights must be left on.

EMERGENCY INFORMATION

Dial 17 for police or ambulance and 18 for fire.

GASOLINE STATIONS

Stations are available throughout France. Unleaded gasoline *(sans plombe)* is sold in many stations on major roads and motorways. The tourist offices have a map showing the locations of these stations.

Motorists driving the world-renowned autobahn experience a thrill that few other roads can offer. (German National Tourist Office)

GERMANY

CAPITAL: Bonn

POPULATION: 78,700,000

AREA: 146,250 square mi/375,000 square km

CURRENCY UNIT: Deutschemark (DM); Pfennige

LANGUAGE: German

TIME FROM UNITED STATES: Eastern Standard plus 6 hours

TELEPHONE ACCESS CODES: to United States, 00 or USA Direct 0130–0010; from United States, 49

EMBASSIES/CONSULATES: *American Embassy,* Deichmanns Avenue, 5300 Bonn 2; phone: (0228) 3391. *American Consulate,* Koniginstrasse 5, Munich; phone: 089 23011. Cleyellee 170, 1000 Berlin 33; phone: (030) 81975. *British Embassy,* 77 Friedrich Ebert Allee, 5300 Bonn 1; phone: (0228) 234061. *British Consulate,* Uhlandstrasse 7/8, 1000 Berlin 12; phone: (030) 309–52–92–4. Amalienstrasse 62, 8000 Munich 40; phone: (089) 39–40–15/9

CONTACTS FOR PRETRIP PLANNING

Automobile Clubs

Allgemeiner Deutscher, Automobil-Club e.V. (ADAC):

Munich: ADAC, 8000 Munich 70, Am Westpark 8; phone: 089/76–76–0. *Frankfurt:* ADAC Hessen e.V., 6000 Frankfurt 1, Schumannstrasse 4-6; phone: 0611/74–30–1. *Hamburg:* ADAC Hansa e.V., 2000 Hamburg 1, Ansinckstrasse 39; phone: 040/28–99–1. *Cologne:* ADAC Nordhein e.V., 5000 Cologne 51, Aeteburger Strasse 375; phone: 0221/37–99–0

Automobilclub von Deutschland e.V. (AvD):

Frankfurt: AvD, Lyoner Strasse 16, D-6000 Frankfurt a.M.-71; phone: 0611/66–06–3000. *Bremen:* AvD-Landesgruppe, Holler Allee 10-12, D-2800 Bremen-1; phone: 0421/34–33–34. *Heidelberg:* AvD Club Kurpfalz, DER-Buro Menglerbau, D-6900 Heidelberg; phone: 06221/2–70–43. *Cologne:* AvD-ACV-Reiseburo GmbH, Johannisstrasse 54, D-5000 Cologne 1; phone: 0221/12–20–03

Munich: Deutscher Touring Automobil-Club, 8 Munich 65, Postfach 140, Munich; phone: 811–1048 or 811–1212

TOURIST OFFICES

United States: German National Tourist Office, 747 Third Avenue, New York, NY 10017; phone: (212) 308–3300. *Britain:* German National Tourist Office, Nightingale Road, 65 Curzon Street, London W1Y 7PE; phone: (071) 495–3990

Germany: Berlin Tourist Office, Europa-Center, Tauentzienstrasse, D-1000 Berlin; phone: (30) 2–12–34. Cologne Tourist Office, Unter Fettenheunen 19, D-5000 Cologne 1; phone: (221) 221–33–40. Frankfurt Tourist Office, Gutleutstrasse 7-9, D-6000 Frankfurt 1; phone: (69) 3–13–36–77. Munich Tourist Office, Postfach, D-8000 Munich 1; phone: (89) 2–39–11

FERRIES

Scandinavia Seaways Ferry Lines: *United States,* EuroCruises (800) 688–EURO; DFDS Travel Center (800) 533–3755 or (305) 491–7909; *Britain,* (0482) 77177 for reservations or 795141 for general inquiries. Routes from Hamburg to Harwich, Travemunde to Helsinki, and Warnemunde to Gedser Odde (Denmark)

Airlines

Lufthansa: *United States,* (800) 645–3880; *Britain,* (071) 408–0442

TOPOGRAPHY

A reunited Germany pulls together one of the world's most remarkable highway systems. The word *autobahn* is almost synonymous with the concept of superhighways, first developed during Hitler's regime and later exported throughout the world. Some of the original autobahns are showing their age—narrow lanes, rough surfaces, curves unsuited for speeds of 80 to 120 mph—but most in the west have been modernized. The east is another story, and a very uneven one: some autobahns, like the main line from Hannover to Berlin, are in immaculate condition, while others, like the east-west link between Dresden and the old border, are appallingly rough. But the main point is the efficiency of a highway network that provides comprehensive coverage of regions in the west and leads to many key regions in the east. And it is sophisticated enough to provide subnetworks around key cities and industrial centers—Berlin, Hamburg, the Ruhr, Frankfurt, and Munich. Autobahns, in fact, radiate in all directions from Berlin, which has a very efficient system of outer and inner ring roads, but the general coverage in the east is far thinner than in the west.

The topography of the country as a whole consists of a layered series of distinct landscapes rising southward from the Baltic and North seas lowlands to the Bavarian alps along the Swiss and Austrian borders. The great plain in the north extends all the way from Hamburg in the west to Berlin and the Polish border in the east. South of a line between Hannover and Berlin, the Hanz, Vogelsberg, Rahn, and Thuringian mountain ranges fill much of the center of Germany. Autobahns cross this area in widely spaced swaths, but most of the mountain driving is on slower secondary

roads. In contrast, a dense network of autobahns blankets western regions of Germany, stretching from the industrial cities of the Ruhr southward through Cologne, Frankfurt, and Mannheim to Stuttgart. This is a busy area to drive through, and sometimes heavy truck traffic totally fills the right lane, effectively reducing the autobahn to a single lane for automobiles.

The main artery of the west is still the Rhine valley, chock full of barges and excursion boats on the water and flanked by highways. Flowing from Switzerland to the North Sea through a sharply cut valley, the Rhine dominates the landscape for tourists, in spite of the noisy medley of major transport. Along its banks, vineyards climb up steep slopes, interspersed with deep gorges dropping to the river and dozens of castles standing on rock outcroppings. Driving along the Rhine through scenery such as this, as well as a string of historic cities and towns, is deservedly popular among tourists. The road on the west bank is fast from Cologne south to Koblenz, then both sides slow down until you reach a big bend just before Wiesbaden. The east bank traces more gorges and is thereby more scenic and slower, although the other gives a broader view of the same sights. For those with a passion for the valley, there's an even slower tourist route that crawls along the heights of the east bank. If you're in the fast lane and haven't time for any scenic route, there is an autobahn just west of the Rhine.

Southern Germany is well served by autobahns heading south toward Heidelberg and Freiburg, southeast toward Stuttgart and Munich, and east toward Nurnberg and Regensberg. But there are many opportunities for drivers who have time to detour into smaller roads and discover the special beauties of regions like the Black Forest, where driving is slow but always rewarding. Farther east, the "Romantic Road" has to be treated with more caution: The northern section between the remarkable medieval towns of Rothenburg, Dinkelsbuhl, and Nordlingen is indeed pastoral and romantic; but farther south, toward Augsburg, it is simply crowded with trucks and dull.

Another touring road called the "German Alpine Road" along the Swiss and Austrian borders from Lindau through Garmisch all the way to Berchtesgaden earns its name all the way by providing a variety of Bavarian mountain scenery, including a circuit around the highest mountain in Germany, the Zugspitze.

ROAD CONDITIONS

The main roads of Germany are in good condition. An extensive network of autobahns provides an efficient means to reach most destinations, but weekend traffic can be heavy, and the unlimited speeds are notorious. With many powerful cars going full bore, watch all three mirrors like a hawk; then you can change lanes in time when a speck from behind zooms up at a speed 50 or 60

Traffic from Kurfurstendamm winds around the Kaiser Wilhelm Memorial Church in the center of Brietscheidplatz, a popular meeting place in Berlin. (Berlin Tourist Office)

miles faster than your cruising speed. Main roads in the Bavarian Alps are open year-round, but there may be delays in bad weather. Two-lane roads, such as along the "Romantic Road" south of Dinklesbuhl, can be slow with lots of truck traffic.

In former East Germany some roads, both in towns and in the country, are made of brick or wooden blocks—they are bumpy and very slow. Often there are no shoulders. Level railroad crossings are frequent, marked by a blinking white light to let drivers know it is working, red to warn of an approaching train. Most towns do not have bypasses, so drivers must go all the way through. Some autobahn sections are rough. The road from Berlin to the west has been resurfaced and is in good condition.

Information on mountain passes:

Achen: 990 meters in height, Route 307 Tegernsee to Jenbach, open in winter

Auersberg: 1,018 meters, open all winter

Fichtelberg: 1,214 meters, open all winter

HIGHWAY SIGNS

European roads are signed with "E" on a green rectangle. Federal roads have black numbers on yellow.

German signs follow international procedure. In addition there are other signs the driver should be aware of. A blue rectangular sign with a white arrow stating EINBAHNSTRASSE means "one-way street." A yellow circular sign with green edge and the letter "H" means "bus or tram stop." A blue circular sign with "30" indicates minimum speed. If there are two numbers, such as "50–70," it means there is a speed range. Either a yellow sign with UM-LEITUNG or a blue sign with "U" marks a detour or diversion. A green-edged triangle with a flying eagle and LANDSCHAFTS SCHUTZGEBIET means that the area is protected, and no parking is allowed. Blue rectangular signs with white arrows indicate which lane to use.

Here are some useful translations of other road signs: *Rollsplitt:* loose grit; *Frostchaden:* frost damage: *Glatteisgefahr:* ice on the road; *Radwegkreutz:* cycle-track crossing; *Strassenschaden:* road damage; *Fahrbahnwechsel:* change traffic lane; *Freie Fahrt:* road clear; *Baustofflagerung:* road works material; *Seitenstreifen nicht befahrbar:* use of shoulder or verge not advised.

DRIVING REGULATIONS

• A valid license from home is required. An International Driving License is recommended but not necessary.

• All German vehicles must carry a first-aid kit; it is also recommended for visitors.

• Drive on the right, pass on the left. At intersections cars from the right have right-of-way. At traffic circles entering vehicles have right-of-way. Special signs indicate other rules on traffic circles; watch for cases where those on the circle have right-of-way.

• Drivers must carry a warning triangle.

• Seat belts are mandatory in the front seat of a vehicle, as well as in the back seat of a vehicle fitted with rear belts. Children under the age of twelve are not allowed to ride in the front seat.

• Speed recommendation is 130 kph/81 mph on autobahns, and the speed limit is 130 kph/81 mph on other roads with at least two lanes in each direction. On roads with only one lane in each direction the speed limit is 100 kph/62 mph. In built-up areas the speed limit is 50 kph/31 mph. The top speed limit in the former GDR is 100 kph/62 mph.

PARKING

Parking is permitted only on the right side of a street, except for one-way streets.

Parking is prohibited less than 5 meters on each side of a pedestrian crossing and less than 10 meters in front of traffic lights.

Parking meters and disks are used.

EMERGENCY INFORMATION

In case of an accident, dial 110.

GASOLINE STATIONS

Stations are available in most of Germany. Prices are higher on autobahns. Unleaded gasoline is marked *bleifrei*.

The Acropolis of Lindos on Rhodes, dating back to the fifth century B.C., towers over a harbor relatively unchanged by time. (Greek National Tourist Office/Meredith Pillon)

GREECE

CAPITAL: Athens (Athinai)
POPULATION: 9,850,000
AREA: 51,476 square mi/131,990 square km
CURRENCY UNIT: Greek drachma (DR)
LANGUAGE: Greek
TIME FROM UNITED STATES: Eastern Standard plus 7 hours
TELEPHONE ACCESS CODES: to United States, 00 or USA Direct
   00–800–1311; from United States, 30
EMBASSIES: *American Embassy,* 91 Vasilissis Sophias Boulevard,
   10160 Athens; phone: 721–2951 or 711–8401. *British Embassy,*
   1 Odos Ploutarchou, Athens 106 75; phone: 72–36–211

CONTACTS FOR PRETRIP PLANNING

Automobile Clubs

Athens: Automobile and Touring Club of Greece (ELPA), 2-4
   Messogion Street, Athens 115 27; phone: 01–7791615. *Iráklion:*
   ELPA, Iráklion, Knossou and Papandreou Avenue, 713 06;
   phone: (081) 289440. *Patras:* ELPA, Patras 127, Astingos and
   Corinthou Streets 262 23; phone: 426416. *Thessaloníki:* ELPA,
   Thessaloníki 228, Vas. Olgas Avenue, 551 33; phone: (031)
   426319

Tourist Offices

United States: Greek National Tourist Organization, 645 Fifth
   Avenue, New York, NY 10022; phone: (212) 421–5777.
   Britain: Greek National Tourist Organization, 4 Conduit Street,
   London W1R PDJ; phone: (071) 734–5997

Greece: Greek National Tourist Organization (G.N.T.O.), 2
   Amerikis Street, P.O. Box 1017, Athens GR-101 10; phone: (01)
   322–3111. G.N.T.O., 1 Xanthoudidou Street, Heraklion; phone:
   (081) 228–203. G.N.T.O., 40 Kriari Street, Hania; phone: (0821)
   26426. G.N.T.O., Venizelou Avenue, Rethymon; phone: (0831)
   29148

Ferries

Ferries are an important mode of transportation here. It is wise to
check schedules *while in* Greece. Interisland ferry service information is posted at island ports on a weekly basis, giving destinations
and schedules. Looking for a car ferry (instead of passengers-
only), as we did, can compound the problem. We had long waits
and inaccurate information when trying, for example, to leave
Crete for Santorini. We were sent from one town on Crete to another just to get the information on car ferries—and the ship was
twenty-four hours late in arriving! We spend an extra night in a
hotel and then sat in our car on the dock for hours, finally boarding after midnight. Finding no cabins available we dozed on
couches in a lounge. It wasn't our most successful venture. (We
understand that passenger ferries run on a more reliable schedule, but please check anyway.)

Adriatica: *United States,* (813) 394–3384; *Britain,* c/o Sealink
   Stena Line (071) 828–8947 or 1940. Routes from Patras, Corfu,
   and Igoumenitsa to Brindisi; Pireas and Crete to Venice and
   Dubrovnik

Afroessa Lines: *United States,* (800) 367–1789 or (213) 544–3551;
   Greece, 418–377. Routes from Piraeus to Rhodes, Limassol, and
   Haifa

Arkadia Line: *United States,* International Cruise Center Inc.
   (800) 221–3254 or Sea Connection Center (800) 367–1789.
   Routes from Rhodes and Piraeus to Limassol, Cyprus

Fragline: *United States,* (800) 221–3254 or (516) 747–8800; *Greece,* 822–1285. Routes from Patras, Igoumenitsa, and Corfu to Brindisi, Italy

Hellenic Mediterranean: *United States,* (415) 989–7434; *Greece,* 417–4341. Routes from Patras to Brindisi

Jadrolinija: *United States,* (800) 221–3254 or (516) 747–8800; *Britain,* c/o Viamare Travel, (081) 452–8231; *Greece,* 452–0244. Routes from Patras, Corfu, and Igoumenitsa to Dubrovnik, Split, and Rijeka, Yugoslavia

Karageorgis: *United States,* (800) 367–1789 or (213) 544–3551; *Greece,* 923–4201. Routes from Patras to Ancona, Italy

Marlines: *United States,* (800) 221–3254 or (516) 747–8800; *Greece,* 411–0777. Routes from Ancona to Igoumenitsa, Patras, Heraklion, and Izmir

Minoan Lines: *United States,* (800) 221–3254 or (516) 747–8800; *Greece,* 7512–356. Routes from Patras, Igoumenitsa, and Corfu to Ancona, Italy; also from Piraeus, Poros, Samos, and Corfu to Ancona, Italy, and Kusadsi, Turkey

Stability Lines: *United States,* (800) 221–3254 or (516) 747–8800; *Greece,* 4132–392. Routes from Piraeus and Rhodes to Heraklion, Crete; Limassol, Cyprus; and Haifa, Israel

Strintzis Lines: *United States,* (800) 367–1789 or (213) 544–3551; *Britain,* c/o Viamare Travel, (081) 452–8231; Greece, 412–9815. Routes from Patras to Igoumenitsa, Corfu, and Ancona, Italy

Ventouris Ferries: *United States,* (800) 221–3254 or (516) 747–8800; *Greece,* 482–8901. Routes from Corfu, Igoumenitsa, and Patras to Bari, Italy

Airlines

Olympic: *United States,* (800) 223–1226; *Britain,* (081) 846–9080

TOPOGRAPHY

The difficulty of getting around mainland Greece has been noted by travelers since ancient times, because much of the land is blocked by mountain barriers or isolated by the sea. The topography is still magnificent but difficult for land travelers, although mountain paths have been replaced by a limited number of good roads. There is only one major motorway; it runs southward from the Yugoslavian border, snaking down the Aegean coast from Thessaloniki to Athens, then turns west toward the Peloponnese and runs along the Gulf of Corinth to Patras, Greece's major ferry port for connections to the west. There is at least one main highway leading through many regions of Greece—from Thessaloniki east to Macedonia and Thrace and west to Epirus and sections of the Ionian coast; from Larissa west and south in Thessaly; and from Corinth and Patras encircling the northern half of the Peloponnese. Most other regions are served by paved secondary roads, beautiful but slow in mountain regions. Many remote areas, particularly in central Greece and the southern Peloponnese, are still roadless or nearly so. Drivers will find that almost all secondary roads go right down the main street of villages, which made perfect sense when they were built; in terrain where villagers are thankful for any road connection, bypasses have little appeal. You'll also share the road in town and out with flocks of goats or sheep sometimes.

Mainland Greece includes Epirus, Macedonia, Thrace, Thessaly, Central Greece (Akarnia, Fokida, Boeotia, Attica), and the Peloponnese. Throughout the whole of this terrain in every direction, drivers will face mountain ranges—in the east in Thrace and Macedonia, and in much of Thessaly, from Mount Olympos extending southward to Ossa, Pelion, and Euboia. In the western part of the mainland the Yugoslavian Alps continue south through the Pindos chain, Mount Epiros, the Ionian Islands, Mount Parnassos, and into the Peloponnese.

Luckily, there are agricultural areas between some of the mountains, allowing temporary respite for drivers. Thessaly contains a fertile plain surrounded by Mounts Pindos, Olympos, Pelion, Ossa, and Timphristos. Attica consists of a plain and low hills filled with olive trees and vineyards. Athens is located in a hollow between Mounts Hymettos, Parnes, and Pentelikon. The Boeotian plain around Thebes is flat, as is the eastern coast of the Peloponnese, the Argolid, and the coastal area from Corinth westward

Lycabettus Hill, the highest point in Athens, provides a panoramic view of the city and the Acropolis. (Greek National Tourist Office/ Meredith Pillon)

to Achaia. And in the center of the Peloponnese, Arcadia is one vast pastureland.

To see the rest of Greece you must become amphibious. The Greek island chains—Ionian, Saronic, Sporades, Cyclades, and Dodecanese—continue some of the same rugged topography under and above the sea as the mountain ranges submerge and reappear. Here drivers take to ferries to cover much of their distance, but if you think touring archipelagos by car is ridiculous, think again before abandoning your car on the mainland. The larger islands—Chios, Lesbos, Rhodes, and, of course, Crete—have extended road systems, and some of the smaller ones have sketchy public transportation. We have driven on many of them and found that having our own wheels enabled us to go where we wished.

ROAD CONDITIONS

It wouldn't be accurate to say that all roads in Greece are in good condition, but at least they are not boring. A majority of the main roads are in good shape, but on at least one of them drivers make an unusual assumption. During our first drive along the main highway from Athens to Corinth, we realized that drivers expect you to move over onto the shoulder as they approach either from behind or head-on! The road is not quite two or four lanes—more like three—and there is a wide shoulder on each side. You had better move over when you see a Greek car approach. You must be wary of any cyclists, motorcycles, or parked cars on the shoulder. This custom perpetuates the dangers of three-lane roads and may produce a few white knuckles on the steering wheel.

Mountain roads are another matter. We may have more stories to tell simply because we have driven in Greece's mountains so much, yet we still have a positive feeling for our rambles and keep going back for more. One year the new Saab we were driving on and off more ferries than we cared to count, even survived a drop from ferry to dock (the ferry was unable to lower its platform all the way). We worried about its tires and the shaking of all its timbers on some of the rough roads we needed to navigate. All was well except that the car had a fire in it after we reached home—we figured that the catalytic converter riding with the spare tire all year had rattled too much. But we will be returning soon—with another new car, leaving its catalytic converter somewhere else.

On the islands where mountain roads make up much of the network, rental cars pose an additional problem. We were unable to make advance arrangements with an uncertain arrival schedule during a three-month voyage. Often we had to take whatever the sometimes-only rental office in town had available. We normally recommend looking over a rental car carefully, but if it is the only one available there isn't much choice. Each car had one defect or another, but we lived with them all, chalking up any incidents to one more learning experience. It's amazing what a driver and passenger can figure out on a dirt road high up in the mountains.

HIGHWAY SIGNS

If you don't read Greek, you can still read street signs in Athens, as well as destination signs on major Greek roads. Names are spelled phonetically in the Latin alphabet. International driving symbols are used throughout Greece. There are now two superhighways, both toll roads: one connecting Athens with Thessaloniki in the north and the other, across the Northern Peloponnese, connecting Athens with Patras to the west.

DRIVING REGULATIONS

- It is recommended that visitors carry an International Driving License.
- Drive on the right, pass on the left. Passing on the right is prohibited. Right-of-way is given to traffic entering from the right. In the country traffic on the main road has right-of-way.

- Drivers and passengers must wear seat belts.
- Drivers must carry a warning triangle, first-aid kit, and fire extinguisher.
- Speed limits on motorways may not exceed 100 kph/62 mph, on other roads 80 kph/50 mph, and in built-up areas 50 kph/30 mph.

PARKING

Parking meters are in use in some areas; it is not permissible to make use of unexpired time on a meter.

In Athens drivers may not park in the "green zone" except at a parking meter.

Drivers may not park within 5 meters of an intersection, stop sign, or traffic light. Parking is not allowed within 3 meters of a fire hydrant or 15 meters of a bus or tram stop. The police may remove your plates if you park in a no-parking zone.

EMERGENCY INFORMATION

Dial 100 for the police or 109 in some suburbs of Athens. For patrol service dial 104.

GASOLINE STATIONS

Stations are located all over Greece, except in sparsely populated mountain areas. Most of the stations also carry unleaded gasoline, labeled *amoliwdi wensina.*

Szechenyi Medicinal and Open-air Baths, built early in this century, contain one of Budapest's many thermal springs. (Ibusz, Hungarian Travel Company)

HUNGARY

CAPITAL: Budapest

POPULATION: 10,710,000

AREA: 36,282 square mi/93,030 square km

CURRENCY UNIT: Hungarian forint (FT)

LANGUAGE: Hungarian

TIME FROM UNITED STATES: Eastern Standard plus 6 hours

TELEPHONE ACCESS CODES: to United States, 00 (await second dial tone) 36–0111; from United States, 36

EMBASSIES: *American Embassy,* V. Szabadsag Ter 12, 1054 Budapest; phone: 112–6450; *British Embassy,* Harmincad Utca 6, Budapest V; phone: 182–888

CONTACTS FOR PRETRIP PLANNING

Automobile Clubs

Budapest: Magyar Autoklub, (MAK) Romer Floris utca. 4/a, B.P.1, 1272 Budapest 11; phone: (1) 152–040

Tourist Offices

United States: Ibusz Hungarian Travel Company, North American Division, One Parker Plaza, Suite 1104, Fort Lee, NJ 07024; phone: (201) 592–8585. *Britain:* Danube Travel Agency, 6 Conduit Street, London W1R 9TG, phone: (071) 493–0263; also, Representative of the Hungarian Republic, 35, Eaton Place, London SW1; phone: 235–7191 or 4048. *Hungary:* Ibusz, 1053 Budapest, VIII, Tanacs Krt. 3/c; phone: 142–3140

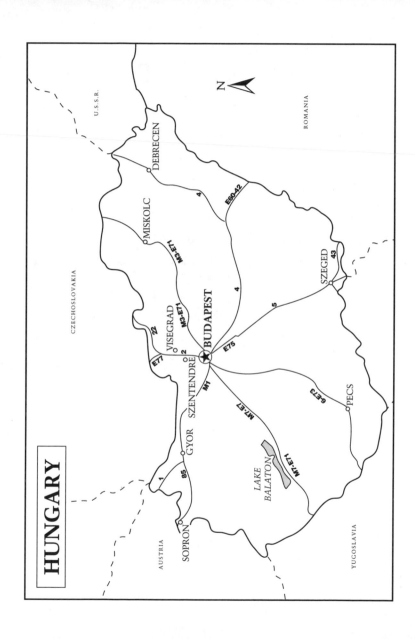

Airlines

Malev: *United States,* (800) 223–6884 or (212) 757–6480; *Britain,* (071) 439–0577; Budapest, 184–333

TOPOGRAPHY

Those unfamiliar with Hungary may be surprised to learn how important water is to the topography of a totally landlocked country. There is a vast reservoir under the ground that spouts up in thermal waters and artesian wells all over Hungary, and Budapest has been famous as a spa city for centuries. But the crucial topographical feature for touring is the Danube River itself: It links Budapest to Vienna upstream and Belgrade downstream and divides Hungary into the Great Plain to the east and the hills of Transdanubia to the west. The Danube enters Hungary from Austria heading east, rushes through a deep gorge in the stretch between Esztergom and Visegrad, then takes a curve to the south through forested mountain slopes. You can take a scenic drive along the right bank all the way from Esztergom into Budapest; if you do, you'll discover that the mighty river is not blue after all, but interesting nevertheless.

Apart from the roadbeds along the full length of the Danube valley, Hungary's road system reminds travelers of the historical importance of Budapest. The main roads are spokes of a wheel leading to and from the capital. The four partially completed motorways extend out from Budapest and link up with the European road network. The M1 heads northwest to Gyor and Austria, the M3 northeast to Gyongyos and Czechoslovakia, the M5 southeast to Kecskemet and the border between Romania and Serbia, and the M7 southwest to Lake Balaton and Slovenia. Eight completed arterial highways fill in more spokes, and link roads connect them to towns in between. This simple and logical system provides good coverage because the country has few internal barriers apart from the Danube.

Transdanubia, or western Hungary, is located south and west of the Danube River. Its hills anticipate the Yugoslavian and Austrian Alps to the west, and the landscape is filled with vineyards, orchards, and farmland. Its major feature is Lake Balaton, the largest lake in central Europe. Motorists can encircle the lake on a road linking resorts or take ferries across the middle. A shallow lake with an average depth of only 2–3 meters (7–10 feet) and milky green water, Balaton warms up quickly in the spring; the south shore, known as the Hungarian Riviera, has sandy beaches stretching the length of the lake. The north shore contains a number of extinct volcanoes; Badacsony, the largest and most spectacular, has grotesque rock formations.

The Millennial Monument, situated on Budapest's Hero's Square, commemorates the thousandth anniversary of the Conquest of Hungary. (Ibusz, Hungarian Travel Company)

East of the Danube all the way to Romania lies the "puszta" or Nagy Alfold, a flat, treeless plain easily explored through secondary roads. Sheep and cattle roam through this grassland, and hunters are attracted by both large and small game, while purple herons, white storks, and spoonbills provide color for bird-watchers. The Tatra Mountains in the north near the Czechoslovakian border, Hungary's major range reaching a thousand meters (3,300 feet), offer spas and an abundance of wineries. The 22-kilometer (14-mile) Aggtelek caverns system lies underground in northeastern Hungary.

ROAD CONDITIONS

Carts, horses, cycles, and tractors are found on many of the roads. Main highways are smooth and straight but without shoulders. Only short stretches of four-lane motorways are completed; more two-lane limited access roads are done.

Utinform is the information center of the highway offices that maintain roads. Its twenty-four-hour service can be reached by calling 227–052 or 227–643. Fovinform provides information on the Budapest road network on 171–173. Callers can receive information on traffic restrictions, road and traffic conditions, and detours. There are no mountain passes that are blocked by winter snow, but chains are recommended for winter travel in the mountains.

HIGHWAY SIGNS

National highways are signed with numbers from 1 to 8. Second-class roads are numbered from 10 to 89. Road signs conform to International standards.

On motorways and major roads, green signs indicate the directions of major towns and give road numbers. The system of signs within towns is not unified; direction signs indicating the centers or the next major road are shown by either a blue, green, or white sign.

Minor roads are dual numbered, the first showing the major road and the second showing its ordinal number. The higher the second number, the farther the road is from the capital. All settlements with a minimum of two hundred inhabitants can be reached by road.

On the pavement a cycle lane is separated from the rest of the road by a continuous yellow stripe. Vehicles are not allowed to drive or stop there.

DRIVING REGULATIONS

• The speed limit in built-up areas is 60 kph/37 mph, on national roads 80 kph/50 mph, and on motorways 100 kph/62 mph. Changes to limits are displayed on signs at the border stations.
• The use of safety belts is obligatory in the front seats. Children under six years of age may not travel in front seats.
• Dimmed headlights must be used from dusk to dawn and in cases of bad visibility.
• In built-up areas horns may be used only when there is danger of an accident.
• Right-of-way at traffic circles is given to vehicles already in motion. Trams and buses have right-of-way in all cases.
• No alcohol is allowed in the blood when driving.
• Auxiliary stop lights are forbidden, as is the use of back-window shades of cloth or foil.
• It is compulsory to have third-party insurance.
• British drivers need an International Driving License.

PARKING

Parking is a worldwide problem. In order to ease the situation, vehicles with an axle weight of less than 1,000 kg are allowed to park on the pavement, providing parking is not forbidden and there is at least 1 meter access for pedestrians.

On main roads parking is permitted on the pavement only where indicated by a continuous white line on the pavement.

Special parking places are allocated to disabled drivers, who may drive and park on roads where general traffic access is forbidden.

EMERGENCY INFORMATION

In case of an accident, dial 07 for police, 05 for fire, and 04 for ambulance.

The State Insurance must be notified within forty-eight hours if a car displaying foreign-number plates has been damaged. The police must be notified and a report of damage obtained for inspection when leaving the country.

GASOLINE STATIONS

Stations are open twenty-four hours around tourist centers, large towns, and at international borders.

Some AFOR and Shell stations carry unleaded gasoline. It can be purchased at about every 100 km (62 mi) along highways and in stations in Budapest. Maps indicating stations are posted at border crossings and in stations. Unleaded gasoline conforms to EEC regulations. It is labeled *olommentes benzin*.

The High Cross and Round Tower in Kells, County Meath, remain on the site of the medieval monastery that produced The Book of Kells, *an illustrated gospel now preserved in the Trinity College Library, Dublin.* (Bord Failte Photo, Irish Tourist Board)

IRELAND

CAPITAL: Dublin

POPULATION: 3,510,000

AREA: 70,282 square mi/179,922 square km

CURRENCY UNIT: Irish punt (IRE) and pence

LANGUAGES: English and Gaelic

TIME FROM UNITED STATES: Eastern Standard plus 5 hours

TELEPHONE ACCESS CODES: to United States, 16; from United States, 353 for the Republic of Ireland, 44 for Northern Ireland

EMBASSIES: *American Embassy,* 42 Elgin Road, Ballsbridge, Ireland; phone: Dublin 68–87–77. *British Embassy,* 33 Merrion Road, Dublin 4; phone: 69–52–11

CONTACTS FOR PRETRIP PLANNING

Automobile Clubs

Dublin: Royal Irish Automobile Club, Dawson Street 34, Dublin, C.2; phone: Dublin 77–51–41 or 75–59–28 or 77–56–28

Tourist Offices

United States: Irish Tourist Board, 757 Third Avenue, New York, NY 10017; phone: (212) 418–0800. *Britain:* Irish Tourist Board, 150 New Bond Street, London W1Y 0AG; phone: (071) 493–3201. Northern Ireland Tourist Board, 11 Berkeley Street, London W1; phone: (071) 493–0601. Northern Ireland Tourist Board, 48 High Street, Belfast, BT1 2DS; phone: (0232) 231221, or tourist information at 246609. *Ireland:* Bord Failte, 14 Upper O'Connell Street, Dublin 1; phone: (01) 747733

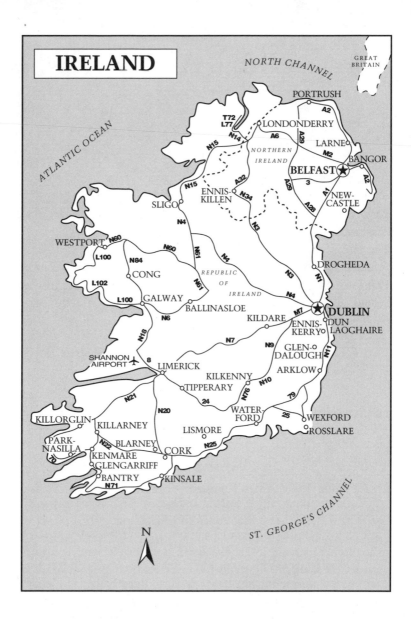

Ferries

B & I Line: *United States,* (800) 221–2474 or (212) 760–0101;
Britain, (071) 734–4681 or 7512 or 3131. Routes from Dublin to
Holyhead, Rosslare to Pembroke Dock

Brittany: *United States,* (800) 221–3254 or (516) 747–8800;
Britain, Portsmouth (0705) 827701, Plymouth (0752) 221321

Caledonian MacBrayne Ltd: *United States,* (800) 221–3254 or
(516) 747–8800; *Britain,* (0475) 33755 or 34531

Irish Ferries: *United States,* (800) 243–8687 or (212) 972–5600.
Route from Rosslare and Cork to Cherbourg and Le Havre

Sealink Stena Line: *Britain,* (0233) 647047. Routes from Rosslare
to Fishguard, Dun Laoghaire to Holyhead, and Larne to Stranraer

Airlines

Aer Lingus: *United States,* (800) 223–6537; Britain, (081) 569–5555

TOPOGRAPHY

There is little evidence of a systematic road pattern in Ireland—
just old roads (connecting towns) that have been straightened out
a bit and paved. Driving in Ireland is quite unaccountably slow on
both main highways and secondary roads, but not because they
are badly designed or maintained; we speculate that the particularly rough surface of otherwise well-paved roads makes drivers
slow down. The net result is that you can be easily fooled when
you look at a map and plan your day's itinerary. We learned to estimate an average speed of no more than a leisurely thirty miles
per hour, which gives travelers all the more time to appreciate
those wonderful shades of green throughout the landscape.

Starting from the ferry port of Rosslare in southeastern Ireland
and moving clockwise, a survey of the coastal perimeter of the

country begins in the pleasant rolling country in County Waterford. Gently rolling hills continue into County Cork. To the west, County Kerry is famous for its lush, almost tropical gardens, where the sea-warmed climate supports plants of Mediterranean origin.

In the southwestern corner of the county three bony-fingered peninsulas stretch out into the sea. Of these the Iveragh is best known to tourists, who may drive its Ring of Kerry on a clockwise route and then return to Killarney. During high season, though, driving on the Kerry Ring can be frustrating because of many tour buses. You might be better off on the Dingle or the Beara; the latter is not as congested because its roads are too small for tour buses.

In the middle of the west coast, County Clare contains the Cliffs of Moher, rising swiftly just north of the surfing beaches at Liscannor Bay to sudden sheer drops into the sea. Also in this county is one of Ireland's geological wonders, and you can drive right into it. The Burren is a tilted plateau with a porous rock crust that looks almost like very rough pavement with Swiss cheese holes. Visitors may think they have landed on the moon as they wander over this hundred square miles of gray limestone filled with fossils and prehistoric graves.

Northwest of Galway long deserted valleys full of peat bogs lead into the mountains and a rugged coastline indented by many rocky bays. Driving is understandably slow in that area. Farther eastward, the whole center of the country is filled with lakes and streams, particularly in the counties of Sligo, Leitrim, Roscommon, Longford, and Westmeath. Fishing and hunting are popular in this region.

The landscape on the eastern side of Ireland is largely verdant, with high rolling hills and even waterfalls in some places. The coast just south of Dublin is a particularly attractive mixture of headlands, coves, beaches, and woods. Farther inland the heavily wooded Wicklow Mountains provide scenery and recreation easily accessible from Dublin by car.

ROAD CONDITIONS

Most of the roads in Ireland are secondary routes, but they are paved. Some roads are narrow by U.S. standards, and drivers may encounter livestock on the roads. Cyclists also make the driver wary. You need to allow more time when driving in Ireland, but this can also lead to unexpected views and a more relaxing trip.

HIGHWAY SIGNS

National primary roads are marked with "N" and a number between 1 and 25. National secondary roads are also marked "N" with numbers above 50. Regional roads are marked "R."

Some road signs are in English and in Gaelic.

DRIVING REGULATIONS

• Drive on the left, and pass on the right, as in England.
• The speed limit is between 64 and 88 kph/40 and 55 mph, according to posted signs on roads outside built-up areas. In cities and towns the speed limit is 48 kph/30 mph.
• Honking horns are not allowed between 11:30 P.M. and 7:00 A.M. on any road that has a speed limit.
• Drivers must carry a driver's license from home or the International Driving License.
• Seat belts are mandatory in Ireland.

PARKING

Watch out for zebra-striped crossings and do not park by the zigzag lines on either side. Parking tickets can be obtained from the machines found along the roads and in parking lots.

EMERGENCY INFORMATION

Dial 999 for emergencies.

GASOLINE STATIONS

Stations are located all over Ireland. Drivers beginning a trip out on one of the peninsulas in the southwest should probably fill up before leaving, as there are stretches of isolated mountain roads.

Unleaded gasoline is labeled "unleaded BS7070 premium."

ITALY

CAPITAL: Rome (Roma)

POPULATION: 57,000,000

AREA: 126,360 square mi/324,000 square km

CURRENCY UNIT: Italian lira (LIT)

LANGUAGE: Italian

TIME FROM UNITED STATES: Eastern Standard plus 6 hours

TELEPHONE ACCESS CODES: to United States, 001 or USA Direct 172–1011; from United States, 39

CONSULATES AND EMBASSIES: *U.S. Consulate,* Via Vespucci, 38, 50123, Florence; phone: (055) 298–276. Banca d'America e d'Italia Building, Piazza Portello, 6, 16134 Genoa; phone: (010) 282–741. Largo Donegani, 1, 20121 Milan; phone: (02) 652–841. Piazza della Repubblica, 80122, Naples; phone: (081) 660–966. *U.S. Embassy,* Via Vittorio Veneto, 121, 00187, Rome; phone: (06) 46741. *British Embassy and Consular Section,* Via XX Settembre 80 A, 00187 Rome; phone: 4755–441/551. *British Consulate,* Lungarno Corsini 2, 1-50123 Florence; phone: 212594. Via San Paolo 7, I-20121 Milan; phone: 869–3442. Vicolo Delle Ville 16, I-34100 Trieste; phone: (040) 302884. Via XII Ottobre 2, 13 Piano, I-16121 Genoa; phone: (010) 564–833/6. Box 679, Dorsodoro (Accademia) 1051, I-30100 Venice; phone: (041) 5227207. Via Francesco Crispi, 122, I-80122 Naples; phone: 663511

CONTACTS FOR PRETRIP PLANNING

Automobile Clubs

Rome: Automobile Club d'Italia Office (ACI), Via Marsala, 8,

00185 Rome; phone: (06) 4998. *Florence:* ACI, Viale Amendola, 36, 50121 Florence; phone: (055) 672813. *Milan:* ACI, Corso Venezia, 43, 20121 Milan; phone: (02) 793966. *Venice:* ACI, Piazzale Roma, 540/B, 30125 Venice; phone: (041) 708828. *Bologna:* ACI, Via Emilia Ponente, 18/2, 40133 Bologna; phone: (051) 387651. *Genoa:* ACI, Viale Brigate Partigiane, 1/a, 16129 Genoa; phone: (010) 566707. *Perugia:* ACI, Via M. Angeloni, 1, 06100 Perugia; phone: (075) 754748

Tourist Offices

United States: Italian Government Tourist Office, also called ENIT, 630 Fifth Avenue, Suite 1565, New York, NY 10111; phone: (212) 245–4822. *Britain:* ENIT, 1 Princes Street, London W1R 8AY; phone: (071) 408–125

Italy: Compagnia Italiana Turismo (CIT), Florence 50121 (Toscana), Via Manzoni, 16; phone: (055) 247–8141/2/3/4/5. CIT, Genoa 16121 (Liguria), Via Roma, 11; phone: (010) 518–407. CIT, Milan (Lombardia), Via Marconi, 1; phone: (02) 870016. CIT, Naples 80121 (Campania), Via Partenope, 10-A; phone: (081) 418–988. CIT Rome 00185 (Lazio), Via Parigi, 11; phone: (06) 461–851. CIT Vicenza 36100 (Veneto), Piazza Duomo, 5; phone: (0444) 544122

Ferries

Adriatica Line: *United States,* (813) 394–3384; *Britain,* c/o Sealink Stena Line, (071) 828–8947 or 1940. Routes from Venice to Losinj, Zadar, Split; Rimini to Pula, Losinj, Zadar; Ancona to Zadar, Split, Dubrovnik; Pescara to Split; Bari to Dubrovnik and Split

The domes and towers on the island of San Giorgio Maggiore mark the sea entrance to the Grand Canal in Venice. (Italian Government Travel Office)

Hellenic Mediterranean Line: *United States,* (415) 989–7434; *Britain,* (071) 499–0076. Routes from Brindisi to Patras, Greece

Jadrolinija: *United States,* (800) 221–3254 or (516) 747–8800; *Britain,* c/o Yugotours, (071) 734–7321 or Viamare Travel (081) 452–8231. Routes from Ancona to Zadar and Split, Yugoslavia; also Bari to Dubrovnik

Karageorgis: *United States,* (800) 367–1789. Routes from Ancona to Patras, Greece

Strintzis: *United States,* (800) 367–1789 or (213) 544–3551; International Cruise Center, Inc., (800) 221–3254; Sea Connection Center, (800) 367–1789; *Britain,* Viamare Travel (081) 452–8231/2. Routes from Ancona to Patras, Igoumenitsa, and Corfu

Tirrenia Line: *United States,* (813) 394–3384; *Britain,* (071) 373–6548/49. Routes from Genoa to Porto Torres, Olbia, Cagliari, Arbatrax; Leghorn to Porto Torres; Civitavecchia to Olbia, Cagliari, Arbetax; Naples to Cagliari; Palermo to Cagliari; Trapani to Cagliari

Ventouris: *United States,* (800) 221–3254 or (516) 747–8800; *Britain,* (071) 409–2760. Routes from Bari to Corfu, Patras

Airlines

Alitalia: *United States,* (800) 223–5730; *Britain,* (071) 602–7111

TOPOGRAPHY

Italy is another country that offers an almost infinite variety of attractions; and they are best seen by car, because an extensive highway system takes you where trains don't go—to volcanoes, hill towns, corniche drives, and archaeological sites.

Italy's autostrada (motorway) system, though not as dense as that of Belgium, Germany, or the Netherlands, is more than adequate to speed you to a string of major cities—Turin, Milan, Verona, Padua, Venice, Bologna, Ravenna, Florence, Rome, Naples—and to lead you into the alps or around Sicily. Its structure is simple and well designed: two long autostrade down the "boot," one on each side, with six connectors crossing the central mountains; a grid of autostrade through the Po Valley; six fingers stretching up into the alps, four of which lead across important passes into adjoining countries; and a partially completed set of autostrade along the coasts and interior valleys of Sicily.

The main line along the west coast links Genoa, Pisa, Florence, Rome, and Naples and extends to the Straits of Messina's ferry ports to Sicily. The east coast autostrada begins in Milan and runs through Parma and Bologna before it reaches the Adriatic, then continues southward through the ferry ports of Ancona and Bari nearly all the way to Taranto. Thus motorways link all the major cities in Italy, and an extensive network of other primary highways and secondary roads leads into the heart of the countryside. Usually it is preferable to zoom along the autostrade to reach the region of your choice, then get on the secondary roads to explore its landscape at a slower pace.

The northern tier is entirely mountainous, continuing the Alps over the borders from France, Switzerland, and Austria. This mountain wall is broken by a number of historically important and once difficult passes—the Great St. Bernard, Mont Blanc, Simplon, St. Gothard, San Bernadino, and Brenner. Upgraded roads and tunnels make visiting these scenic places easier.

South of the high Alps, deep mountain valleys gouged by glaciers filled with water, forming Lombardy's justly famed lake district, which stretches from the Swiss border nearly to Milan. The long, narrow Italian lakes—Maggiore, Lugano, Como—unite the beauty of Switzerland with the softness of a Mediterranean climate. Twisty, slow roads with spectacular views line their shores; drive them with an eye on your mirrors as local drivers are not usually patient with gazing tourists.

The Cathedral in Amalfi stands in splendor at the midpoint of one of Italy's most spectacular corniche drives. (Italian Government Travel Office)

South of the mountains and lakes the central tier of the remarkably fertile Po Valley begins in the uplands of the Piedmont surrounding Turin, then levels out as the river moves through southern Lombardy and Emilia Romagna to its delta bulging into the Adriatic east of Ferrara. The flat Po Valley, normally easy to drive, has frequent and sometimes very dense fog; it is also a major truck route, with consequent air pollution.

To the east of the Po Delta, the shallow lagoons and flat beaches of Venezia stretch along the Adriatic all the way to Trieste and the Yugoslavian border. In the west, across the boot from Venice and just south of the Po Valley, lies the contrasting maritime environment of the Italian Riviera, a playground for centuries. Its mountainous coastline, with headlands sheltering rocky coves and beaches that are a photographer's dream, is best appreciated from the high autostrade along the Adriatic on both sides of Genoa. Farther inland, the Arno flows through Florence and Pisa. Its valley is surrounded by hillside vineyards and small mountains that are well worth exploring on secondary roads; you will see nothing of them from the autostrada.

Just south of Florence the first segments of the Apennines begin marching down the length of Italy into Sicily. Their foothills fill Umbria and Marche, where fortified hill towns perch in improbable places. Your car will treat you to one more hill town to discover and add to your collection; we found our favorites by meandering. The mountains reach their highest point (9,560 feet) in the Gran Sasso massif of Abruzzo, a rugged wilderness area northeast of Rome; the city itself is surrounded by a flatter coastal plain.

The Bay of Naples is the center of the volcanic region in Campania; it still lives under the shadow of Vesuvius. We remember mistakenly driving up the back way (southern road) toward the lip of the crater in our top-heavy camper, which tilted precariously on a road covered with shifting lava. We climbed the last section on foot to reach a narrow ledge where there were no guard rails protecting anyone from falling into that bottomless pit, still eerie with wisps of white smoke. (Most people drive up the graded main route, which is properly fenced at the top.)

Just as interesting is the coastal landscape of the Sorrento peninsula, which contains the justly famed Amalfi Drive, a corniche road that is not as hard to drive as we once thought. Don't try it if you're in a hurry though, because the delicate balance of traffic flow can be stopped by the slightest accident or intrusion of road work. Cliff walks, rock formations and sea caves on the islands of Ischia and Capri at the northern and southern ends of the Bay of Naples can be reached by ferry; a car is useful on Ischia but not as much on Capri.

South of Naples, the autostrada continues through the hills of Campania and high massif of Calabria to the Straits of Messina. Across the strait in Sicily, most of the east coast, from Messina through Taormina and Catania, is dominated by Mount Etna at 10,960 feet; the fabled volcano has many mouths and is still very much alive. You can drive part way to the top on a paved road which is periodically cut by lava flows that are easily spotted along the shoulders. Recent eruptions have destroyed a giant piece of the road and twisted the chair lift stanchions like spaghetti, closing the upper sections of the mountain to visitors except by guided mini-buses. The archeological sites in the southern part of the island are more easily accessible along a flatter coastline. Ferries will take you to two groups of volcanic islands that surround Sicily, the Egadi and Lipari, but you won't need to bring your car unless you are staying for a spell on the larger ones.

ROAD CONDITIONS

Roads are classified as follows: *autostrade* (superhighways), *strade statali* (state roads), *strade provinciali* (provincial roads) and *strade comunali* (local roads).

On a recent trip through Italy, we studied current road conditions. Autostrade link all of the major cities in Italy. Along the Ligurian coast, and elsewhere, they include a series of tunnels wherever the mountains meet the sea. Lighting varies inside the tunnels; some have none at all. On two-lane main highways, smelly trucks pass each other and hold up all of the other drivers. Sometimes it is preferable to zoom along the autostrade to the region of your choice and then get off to explore secondary roads. Since the first year we lived and drove in Italy, in the sixties, the secondary roads have improved considerably. Once the small roads were dirt, full of bumps and dust; now most are paved and kept in good condition. The going may be slow in the mountains, but what views to contemplate!

In most cities, including Milan, Rome, and Naples, it makes sense to park your car and walk or use public transportation. Driving in the cities of southern Italy is precarious at best and sometimes even hair-raising in Naples, where residents abandon all normal restraint. Some drivers ignore red lights, drive on the sidewalks, and zoom around each other, crisscrossing through wide intersections. As an alternative to driving in Naples, stay on Ischia or the Sorrento Peninsula and take the *aliscafi* (catamaran or hydrofoil) for fast commuting to the city. Venice, of course, has no traffic or roads but does present a parking problem; we usually choose to stay outside of the city and take a bus and boat in rather than leave a loaded car beckoning thieves in the parking facility at Mestre.

We strongly recommend thinking twice about taking a long trip on a holiday weekend. We remember spending a very long afternoon at the end of Easter weekend just sitting in our car on the Amalfi Drive. Usually cars whiz around one another with honking and squealing tires, but on that day everyone sat, with much honking and impatience. We chuckled, as we had a front-row seat for a drama played out by two bus drivers and assorted other motorists. It became obvious that the buses could not pass each other going different directions on a hairpin curve. Neither one would give, so they both got out and began shouting, waving their arms around and looking as if they would kill. Other drivers got out of their cars and also yelled, glowered, and gestured. Finally, someone more persuasive than everyone else formulated a plan and convinced one of the bus drivers to back up; of course that had to be preceded by all of the cars behind him backing up. As people left the scene, they waved at one another, animosity forgotten. Today, the Amalfi Drive is as beautiful as ever but still has its quota of wild passers and zoomers who want everyone to move over and let them through hairpin curves.

Information on mountain passes:

Aprica: 1,181 meters high, Route 39 Edolo to Tresenda, closed December–April

Bernina: 2,323 meters, Route 29 Celerina to Tirano, closed November–mid-May

Brenner: 1,380 meters, Routes 182/12 Innsbruck to Bolzano, usually open; autobahn A13/A22 Innsbruck to Bolzano, usually open

Campiglio: 1,514 meters, Route 42 Timani to Dimaro, intermittent closure

Campolongo: 1,874 meters, Route 244 Corvara to Arabba, intermittent closure

Col di Tenda: 1,321 meters, Route N201 La Giandola to Borgo S. Dalmazzo, S20 Tunnel at summit, intermittent closure

Costalunga: 1,753 meters, Route 241 Cortina to Bolzano, intermittent closure

Falzarego: 2,105 meters, Route 48 Ora to Cortina, intermittent closure November–June

Fugazze: 1,161 meters, Route 46 Rovereto to Vicenza, intermittent closure

Gardena: 2,120 meters, Route 243 Selva to Corvara, closed December–April

Gavia: 2,621 meters, Route 300 Bormio to Ponte di Legno, closed December–May

Great St. Bernard: 2,469 meters, Routes 21/27 Martigny to Aosta, closed October–June except through tunnel

Larche: 1,991 meters, Route 21 Cuneo to Barcelonnette, closed November–May

Maloja: 1,815 meters, Route 3 Chiavenna to Silvaplana, intermittent closure

Maura: 1,298 meters, Route 52 Pieve di Cadore to Piani, intermittent closure

Mt. Cenis: 2,083 meters, Route N6 Chambery to Turin, closed late November–late May

Monte Giovo: 2,093 meters, Route Merano to Vipiteno, closed November–early May

Mt. Genèvre: 1,854 meters, Routes N94/24 Briançon to Turin, usually open

Petit St. Bernard: 2,188 meters, Route N90 Bourg-St.-Maurice to Aosta

Plocken: 1,360 meters, Routes 110/52B Kotshach Mauthen to Tolmezzo, usually open

Pordoi: 2,239 meters, Route 48 Arabba to Canazei, closed November–May

Reisa: 1,510 meters, Routes 315/40 Landeck to Malles, usually open

Rolle: 1,972 meters, Route 50 Predazzo to Primiero, closed November–May

Sella: 2,213 meters, Route 242 Ortisei to Canazei, closed December–June

Sestriere: 2,033 meters, Route 23 Cesana Torinese to Turin, usually open

Simplon: 2,005 meters, Route 9 Brig to Domodossola, intermittent closure; there is an alternative rail tunnel for your car from Brig to Iselle

Splugen: 2,115 meters, Route 36 Splugen to Chiavenna, closed November–June

Stelvio: 2,758 meters, Route 38 Bormio to Spondigna, closed mid-October–late June

Timmelsjoch: 2,474 meters, Routes 186/466 Otz to Merano, closed October–end of May

Tonale: 1,884 meters, Route 42 Edolo to Bolzano, closed December–April

Tre Croci: 1,809 meters, Route 48 Cortina to Auronzo, closed November–May

Umbrail: 2,501 meters, Route 66 Santa Maria to Bormio, closed late October–mid-June

HIGHWAY SIGNS

The Italian highway code follows the Geneva Convention, and Italy uses international road signs.

Knowing the translation of the following signs could prove more than just helpful: *Senso Vietato:* no entry; *Vietato Ingresso Veicoli:* no entry for vehicles; *Sosta Autorizzata:* parking permitted (followed by times); *Sosta Vietata:* no parking; *Vietato Transito Autocarri:* closed to heavy vehicles; *Passaggio a Livello:* level crossing; *Rallentare:* slow down; *Svolta:* bend; *Incrocio:* intersection or cross roads; *Uscita:* exit; *Entrata:* entrance; *Lavori in Corso:* road works

DRIVING REGULATIONS

- Drive on the right, pass on the left. Passing on the right is allowed when the car ahead has signaled a left turn and moved to the center of the road, or where travel in parallel rows is permitted.
- Speed limit in cities and towns is 50 kph/31 mph, on main and local roads 90 kph/56 mph, and on highways 130 kph/81 mph. Speed on highways is reduced to 110 kph/68 mph during the following period around the clock; Saturday to Sunday, from Thursday before Easter to the following Wednesday; on every national holiday falling midweek; December 20–January 7; from the Saturday before the second Sunday in July to the first Sunday of September.
- On three-lane roads the middle lane is reserved for passing, which must always be signaled in advance with the directional signal, and kept on while passing. In towns or city traffic on roads with three lanes, or on roads with three or more lanes in each direction, cars are allowed to move in parallel rows.
- At a crossroad motorists must yield to vehicles coming from their right. Streetcars and trains always have the right-of-way from either left or right. At a crossroad marked by a right-of-way or precedence sign (triangle with point downward) or a stop sign, the motorist must yield to all vehicles coming from both right and left.
- Pedestrians have the right-of-way at zebra-striped crossings.
- Seat belts are compulsory.
- U.S. driver's licenses are valid in Italy if you are driving your own car, but the license must be accompanied by a translation. An International Driving License is required when driving rental cars. For motorists not in possession of an IDL, the ACI will issue a declaration upon presentation of a U.S. license. The declaration is obtainable at any ACI Frontier or Provincial Office for a small fee.
- Insurance for all vehicles is compulsory in Italy. A Green Card (Carta Verde) or Frontier Insurance valid for fifteen, thirty, or forty-five days should be issued to cover your car before your trip

to Italy. If you are in Italy beyond forty-five days, you must have a standard Italian insurance policy.

• Dimmed lights must be used at night when approaching on-coming traffic.

PARKING

Parking is permitted on the right-hand side of the road every-where outside cities and towns except on highways, at cross-roads, and on curves and hills not allowing full visibility. If a car is stalled blocking the road because of mechanical difficulty or for any other reason, the driver is required to warn other vehicles by placing a special triangular danger signal at least 30 meters (99 feet) behind. All cars must be equipped with these portable signals, which can be rented in any ACI office for a nominal deposit.

When a stationary vehicle is not clearly visible, parking lights must be kept on.

EMERGENCY INFORMATION

In case of breakdown dial 116, and the ACI will respond to your call. Dialing 113 will bring the police, fire brigade, or an ambulance.

GASOLINE STATIONS

Stations are located all over Italy. In large towns you'll find self-service stations, where payment can be made into a machine after hours.

Gasoline coupons may be purchased at the border at any ACI office or ENIT offices in Europe. Payment for coupons must be made in foreign currency, and coupons are available only to visitors driving cars with a non-Italian registration. Some of the border offices may not be open when you get there. You can receive only one part of three sections of coupons (1: Northern Italy; 2: Southern Italy; 3: Sicily) when you enter Italy, although you must pay for any other sections you want at the border. Then it is necessary to redeem the others when you reach another section (it appears that the government wants to be sure travelers are really driving in the southern part of the country, not only traveling in the north and then perhaps illegally selling extra coupons to someone else). The hitch is that not all regional offices in southern Italy carry the coupons beyond the high season. Recently we drove to four offices before we found one that had them in stock.

Unleaded gasoline is labeled *super senza* or *super bleifri*.

LUXEMBOURG

CAPITAL: Luxembourg
POPULATION: 367,000
AREA; 1,009 square mi/2,587 square km
CURRENCY UNIT: Luxembourg franc and centimes
LANGUAGES: Luxembourgeois, French, German
TIME FROM UNITED STATES: Eastern Standard plus 6 hours
TELEPHONE ACCESS CODES: to United States, 00; from United
States, 352
EMBASSIES: *American Embassy,* 22 Boulevard Emmanuel-Servais,
L-2535 Luxembourg; phone: 46–01–23. *British Embassy,*
15 Boulevard Roosevelt, B.P. 874, L-2018 Luxembourg Ville;
phone: 29864/6

CONTACTS FOR PRETRIP PLANNING

Automobile Clubs

Automobile Club du Grand-Duché de Luxembourg (ACL), 8007
Bertrange, 13 route de Longway, Luxembourg City; phone:
450045

Tourist Offices

United States: Luxembourg National Tourist Office, 801 Second
Avenue, New York, NY 10017; phone: (212) 370–9850.
Britain: Luxembourg National Trade and Tourist Office, 36-37
Picadilly, London W1V 9PA; phone: (071) 434–2800.

Luxembourg: Office National du Tourisme du Grand Duché de
Luxembourg, 77, rue d'Anvers, B.P. 1001, L-1010 Luxembourg;
phone: 40–08–08, or 48–79–99. Syndicat d'Initiative et de

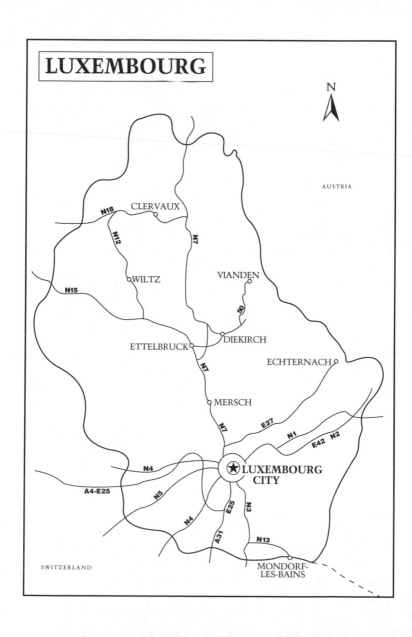

Tourisme, Ville de Luxembourg, B.P. 181, Place d'Armes,
L-2011 Luxembourg; phone: 22809/27565

Airlines

Icelandair: *United States,* (800) 223–5500; Britain, (071) 388–5599

TOPOGRAPHY

Luxembourg is a wonderful entry point for beginning a European
tour because it is centrally located and the driving is easy. The
roads are good and the terrain is rolling without unusual natural
hazards. In the past we have taken delivery of a car in Luxembourg and then scurried on the way to our base of operations for
the year. Recently we had the chance to spend a week in Luxembourg and wondered why we hadn't stopped before. The Duchy
is a miniature of much of the best of the continent; it packs a lot
within its borders.

There is only one motorway, brushing through the southwestern corner of the country to connect Luxembourg City with
France and Belgium. In a familiar pattern, other major highways
radiate from the capital city to the near corners of the realm. In
between, almost every small valley and mountain of this truly
beautiful country can be reached easily and quickly by secondary
roads, and the riverbed drives along the Sure and the Moselle are
particularly attractive.

The topography of Luxembourg divides into two distinct areas.
In the north the "Oesling" is part of a slate mountain range of the
Ardennes. "Little Switzerland" is popular for a driving tour as well
as for hikes on trails in the mountains and through the valleys.
Within an hour or two motorists can visit Vianden's feudal fortress
high on a hill, Echternach's deep chasm, called Wolf Gorge, and
Cleopatra's Needle nearby. There are unusual rock formations in
the forest around Berdorf, and walking tours are clearly marked
there.

The south of the country is called Gutland (good land), and its vineyards cover rolling hills sloping down to the Moselle River. It's pleasant to combine a drive with wine tasting. Near the southern border Mondorf-les-Bains contains thermal springs that draw visitors to cure a variety of ailments.

ROAD CONDITIONS

Roads in Luxembourg are in good condition. Most of them are surfaced with asphalt and are usable year-round.

HIGHWAY SIGNS

Motorway signs follow the international code.

An ancient bridge traverses the gorge at Luxembourg City.
(Luxembourg Travel Office/Jean Proess)

DRIVING REGULATIONS

- Drive on the right, and pass on the left.
- Drivers must carry a current driver's license from home and the current registration certificate for the car.
- Drivers of a vehicle with foreign registration must comply with conditions relating to age and capacity named in the laws of the country of registration.
- Use of a horn is restricted to emergency situations.
- In built-up areas the speed is limited to 60 kph/37 mph, outside these to 90 kph/55 mph, and on motorways to 120 kph/75 mph. Exceptions are signaled.
- Wearing a seat belt is compulsory.
- Insurance regulations are very specific, and some broad European coverages do not meet requirements for underwriters; check your Green Card to make sure your policy is valid in Luxembourg.

PARKING

Parking in blue zones is allowed only with a properly displayed parking disk. Parking meters are also in use. Special parking places are assigned for disabled persons (wheelchair symbol). "Park and ride" lots are located outside of the city of Luxembourg.

EMERGENCY INFORMATION

Dial 012 for police, fire, and ambulance. Road service is provided by the Automobile Club, at 45–00–45.

GASOLINE STATIONS

Stations are located throughout Luxembourg. Unleaded gas is labeled *sans plomb*.

A windmill seemingly floats on a sea of tulips. Flowers and mill alike are synonymous with the Netherlands. (Netherlands Board of Tourism)

THE NETHERLANDS

CAPITAL: Amsterdam
POPULATION: 14,892,574
AREA: 16,052 square mi/41,160 square km
CURRENCY UNIT: guilder (HFL)
LANGUAGE: Dutch
TIME FROM UNITED STATES: Eastern Standard plus 6 hours
TELEPHONE ACCESS CODES: to United States, 09 or USA Direct 06
    (await second dial tone) 022–9111; from United States, 31
EMBASSIES: *American Embassy,* Lange Voorhout 102, The Hague;
    phone: (070) 362–49–11. *British Embassy,* Lange Voorhout 10
    2514ED, The Hague; phone 64–58–00

CONTACTS FOR PRETRIP PLANNING

Automobile Clubs

The Hague: Koninklijke Nederlandse Toeristenbond (ANWB)
    (Royal Dutch Touring Club), Wassenaarseweg 220, 2596 EC
    The Hague; phone: (070) 3147147. *Amsterdam:* ANWB,
    Museumplein 5, Amsterdam; phone:(020) 730844. *Apeldoorn:*
    ANWB, Loolaan 35, Apeldoorn; phone: (055) 21–37–10.
    Arnhem: ANWB, Willemsplein 6, Arnhem; phone: (085)
    45–45–41. *Haarlem:* ANWB, Stationsplein 70, Haarlem; phone:
    (023) 31–91–63. *Leiden:* ANWB, Stationsweg 2, Leiden; phone:
    (071) 14–62–41. *Maastricht:* ANWB, Kiningsplein 60, Maas-
    tricht; phone: (043) 62–06–66. *Rotterdam:* ANWB, Westblaak
    210, Rotterdam; phone: (010) 414–00–00. *Utrecht:* ANWB, Van
    Vollenhoven laan 227, Utrecht; phone: (030) 91–03–33. *Zwolle:*
    ANWB, Tesselschadestraat 155, Zwolle; phone: (038) 536–363

NETHERLANDS

Tourist Offices

United States: Netherlands Board of Tourism, 355 Lexington Avenue, New York, NY 10017; phone: (212) 370–7367. *Britain:* Netherlands Board of Tourism, 25–28 Buckingham Gate, London SW1E 6LD; phone: (071) 630–0451. *Netherlands:* VVV Amsterdam Tourist Office, P.O. Box 3901, 1001 As Amsterdam; phone: 020 26–62–44

Ferries

North Sea Ferries: *United States,* (800) 221–3254 or (516) 747–8800 or through DFDS, (800) 533–3755; *Britain,* (0482) 77177 for reservation or (0482) 795141 for general inquiries; *Amsterdam–Gothenberg,* (305) 491–7909. Route from Rotterdam to Kingston-upon-Hull

Olau Ferry Lines: *Britain,* (0795) 666666; route from Vlissingen to Sheerness

Sealink Stena Line: *Britain,* (0233) 647047; route from Hook of Holland to Harwich

Airlines

KLM: *United States,* (800) 777–5553; *Britain,* (081) 750–9000.

Martinair: *United States,* (800) FON HOLLAND; *Britain,* (0784) 250251

TOPOGRAPHY

The motorway system in the Netherlands is one of the most complete in Europe, with a density to match the population. South of the main line between Amsterdam, Arnhem, and the industrial cities of the Ruhr not far over the German border, the grid of motorways is virtually complete, connecting all cities and most towns of any consequence, as well as providing many links to Germany and Belgium. In North Holland, the new lands reclaimed from the sea, and the eastern and northern provinces, the system is less dense, but so is the population; you can still reach all the major cities—Apeldoorn, Enschede, Zwolle, Leeuwarden, and Groningen—by motorway.

Having said all this, we strongly recommend that you leave this wonderful motorway system and take to the secondary roads if you want to see much of the Netherlands. On the big roads the highway engineering is so good that it bypasses almost everything of interest that might make you slow down and take a look, while smoothly paved secondary roads lead you through an incomparable network of canals and beautiful villages in the western half of the country and equally beautiful but less watery rolling farmland and woods in the eastern half.

Working drawbridges such as this one are numerous in the city of Haarlem. (Netherlands Board of Tourism)

The northern provinces of Friesland, Groningen, and Drenthe contain lakes, canals, and marshes within national parks that attract many vacationers seeking unspoiled land. Be warned that there will be occasional road delays as bridges are opened for boats to pass through. The Frisian Islands, a remarkable barrier of shifting sands off the North Sea coast, are known for bird watching and "mud-walking" and are reached by car ferries.

Much of the center of the Netherlands is sea transformed into lake or land by industrious Dutch hydraulic engineering. Once-seaside villages in North Holland are inland ports on enclosed sections of the old Zuider Zee called the Ijsselmeer and Markermeer, where the water is now fresh instead of brackish. Other former seaports, particularly in Flevoland, are marooned in the middle of new land. Briefly, the story of reclaiming land is as follows: An area is walled off from the sea with dikes, the water pumped out by use of many windmills, and then the land is dried, planted, and cultivated. Roads through the newly reclaimed land are either raised on former dikes or on the sea bottom. Enjoy driving underwater.

The eastern provinces, Overijssel and Gelderland, afford different pleasures for touring. The Ijssel Valley is a wonderful place for cycling, walking, and driving beside orchards, forests, parks, and canals, with brief sidetrips to see unpretentious but immaculately maintained country houses. In the center of Gelderland, between Apeldoorn and Arnhem, lies De Hoge Veluwe, a remarkable national park that features a chateau, a world-famous art museum, and wilderness. The park is well worth a detour from the motorways that whiz right by it.

Most visitors are aware of the mix of canals, streets, and bridges in Amsterdam, but they may not appreciate the logic of its design. The layout of the old city has an interesting semicircular symmetry, with concentric rings and radii of canals bridged by intersecting streets in an amphibious mixture. Most motorists will want to park their cars and move about on canal boats or canalside footpaths.

ROAD CONDITIONS

Roads are well maintained and in good condition without excessive gradients to worry about. Cyclists have a lane on each side of most main roads.

HIGHWAY SIGNS

The green "E" symbol is displayed along international highways linking the Netherlands and its neighbors. The red "A" symbol denotes national highways. Other roads are marked by yellow signs with the letter "N."

DRIVING REGULATIONS

• Drive on the right side, and pass on the left. Drivers should yield right-of-way to traffic approaching from the right, with the exception of major intersections and along roads with right-of-way. Traffic entering a traffic circle has right-of-way.
• On motorways the speed limit is 120 kph/75 mph unless signposted otherwise. Outside built-up areas the maximum speed is 80 kph/50 mph and in built-up areas 50 kph/31 mph.
•Drivers should carry a valid national driver's license from home and valid registration papers for the car.
• Insurance in the form of the Green Card is required. Drivers can obtain temporary insurance coverage for at least fifteen days from the border currency-exchange offices.
• Vehicles must show an international identity disk.

PARKING

Parking meters are used in towns, and parking disks may be obtained from the police, the ANWB, and gasoline stations.

EMERGENCY INFORMATION

To call the police, ambulance, or fire brigade dial 06–11

GASOLINE STATIONS

Stations are located everywhere in the Netherlands. Unleaded gasoline is labeled *loodvrije benzine*.

The Hanseatic Quays and the square-rigger Statsraad Lehmkuhl *lure many to Bergen harbor in Norway's Fjord Country.* (Norwegian National Tourist Office)

NORWAY

CAPITAL: Oslo

POPULATION: 4,158,000

AREA: 126,934 square mi/325,471 square km

CURRENCY UNIT: Norwegian krone (NOK) and Ore

LANGUAGE: Norwegian

TIME FROM UNITED STATES: Eastern Standard plus 6 hours

TELEPHONE ACCESS CODES: to United States, 095 or USA Direct 050–12–011; from United States, 47

EMBASSIES: *American Embassy,* Drammensveien 18, N-0255 Oslo 2; phone: (2) 448550; *British Embassy,* Thomas Heftyesgate 8, Oslo 2; phone: 55–24–00

CONTACTS FOR PRETRIP PLANNING

Automobile Clubs

Oslo: Norwegian Automobile Club (NAF), Storgaten 2, N-0155 Oslo, 1; phone: (02) 42–94–00

Tourist Offices

United States: Norwegian Tourist Board, 655 Third Avenue, New York, NY 10017; phone: (212) 949–2333. *Britain:* Norwegian Tourist Board, 5-11 Charles House, Lower Regent Street, London SW1 4LR; phone: (071) 839–6255. *Norway:* Oslo Tourist Information, Radhuset, N-0158 Oslo 1; phone: (2) 33–43–86

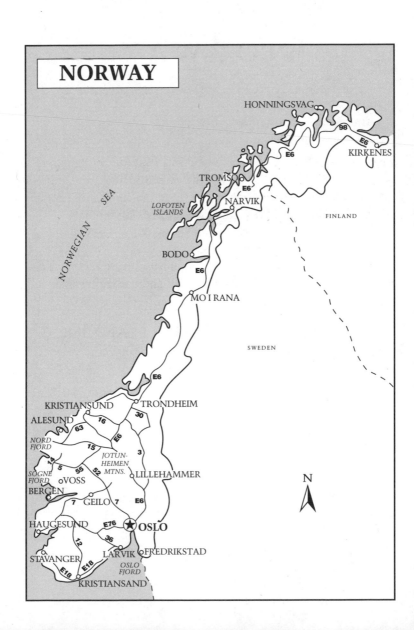

Ferries

Color Line (once Norway Line and Jahre Line, now merged):
United States, c/o Bergen Line, (800) 323–7436 or (212)
986–2711; *Britain,* (091) 296–1313. Routes from Bergen/Sta-
vanger to Amsterdam, and Oslo to Kiel

Scandinavian Seaways: *United States,* EuroCruises
(800) 688–EURO; through DFDS Travel Center (800) 533–3755
or (305) 491–7909; *Britain* (0255) 240240. Route from Oslo to
Copenhagen

Coastal steamers: Three of eleven take cars; *United States,* (800)
221–3254; *Britain,* Norwegian State Railways Travel Bureau
(NSR), (071) 930–666

Airlines

SAS: *United States,* (800) 221–2350; Britain, (071) 734–4020

TOPOGRAPHY

From beyond the Arctic Circle to the southern tip of the Scandinavian Peninsula, Norway stretches its fingers into the sea and
puts its head in the clouds. Majestic seems to be the word for a
country filled with fjords, waterfalls, glaciers, forests, and mountains—all on a large scale.

One can hardly imagine more difficult terrain for highway engi-
neers to deal with—not just mountains dropping into the sea as in
Greece, Norway's closest counterpart, but mountains and fjords
repeatedly interrupting major routes. Boats and skis provide the
natural way to get around, so much so that Norwegians refer to
the mailboat that links Stavanger, Bergen, Trondheim, and the
North Cape as "Highway 1." When they started building railroads
and highways, they took on fearsome engineering tasks and produced some marvels like the truly spectacular rail link between
Oslo and Bergen, Norway's two largest cities, or the rapid drop
from the heights of the Hardangervidda through Mabodalen to

the Eidfjord on the road between the same two cities. So it is not surprising that much of the driving in Norway is slow—a fact that is immediately noticeable when you enter from Sweden, where terrain that is on average gentler permits building faster roads.

In spite of its great natural obstacles, Norway's highways will get you most places you want to go. In the west driving almost always involves taking ferries, which are usually frequent on main highways between major cities but not always so elsewhere. As you head south, where many roads linking with ferries are carved into fjord walls, don't underestimate the driving time. Most of these roads have an unending series of sharp curves, and some are too narrow for opposing traffic to pass in places; you won't enjoy the gorgeous scenery unless you can putter along at an average of 25 miles per hour.

The blend of land and sea on a grand scale stretches from Stavanger northward through Bergen all the way to Trondheim. The southernmost fjordland, Rogaland, is famous for Pulpit Rock, Lysefijord's 600-meter towering cliff with a flat top. A road with almost countless curves climbs from the fjord up into the mountains.

In Hordaland visitors can travel far inland on or beside the Hardangerfjord and explore its upper reaches by car ferry and foot. Just inland is the high mountain plateau of the Hardangervidda, where the barren, rocky landscape has an unforgettable grandeur and the snow lasts well into the summer. You're not likely to miss this experience if you're driving from Oslo to Bergen, since the direct highway between the two cities passes over the Hardangervidda. But don't count on driving that road in the late fall, winter, or early spring when it is piled high with snow.

Farther north the Sognefjord, the longest in Norway, stretches inland more than a third of the way to Sweden. The Jostedalsbreen Glacier, the largest in Europe, lies between the Sognefjord and the Nordfjord. The latter is alive with water flowing down from the glacier and provides another access to it. Cars can drive almost right to the glacier. Our children could hardly believe their luck as they walked on a real glacier one summer.

The far north is another world. From May through August the sun shines twenty-four hours a day beyond the Arctic Circle. Hammerfest is the most northerly town in the world, and beyond it the North Cape ends with soaring granite cliffs 1,000 feet high. To get there, one must choose between the rigors of a long road trip and the more expensive ease of a steamer. You can drive all the way up through the North Cape to the Soviet border, but there is only a single main highway north of Trondheim; needless to say, you must watch your gas supply in this territory.

ROAD CONDITIONS

Roads are well maintained in spite of Norway's winter weather. Some of them are narrow in the mountains. Although most main roads are covered with asphalt, some secondary roads have a gravel surface and may suffer during the spring thaw. The E6 is now asphalt all the way to Kirkenes in the north. A tunnel has replaced a steep section on the road from Gudvangen to Stalheim; the old road is still open as well. Some roads are closed for short periods by snow, and others are closed for the winter, as in much of the western fjord country. From mid-October to late May, the road from Bergen to Oslo via Haukeli is open, but via Eidford and Geilo it is closed. Motorists can also make this trip via a spectacular route through Voss, Gudvangen (ferry to Revsnes), Laerdal, and Fagernes. The road from Oslo to Stavanger is open. The following roads are not open year-round; tentative dates are given when they are closed, subject to weather conditions.

Road no. 5, Gaularfjellet: late December–mid-May
Road no. 7, Hardangervidda: late January–late April
Road no. 13, Vikafjell: late January–late April
Road no. 45, Hunnedalsvegen: open all year
Road no. 51, Valdresflya: late November–late April
Road no. 55, Sognefjellsvegen: early December–mid-May
Road no. 58, Highway 15–Geiranger: end of October–end of May

Road no. 63, Trollstigen: late October–late May
Road no. 95, Skarsvaag–Nordkapp: late October–late April
Road no. 98, Ifjordfjellet: late November–mid-May
Road no. 220, Venabygdfjellet: late February–mid-March
Road no. 252, Tyin–Eidsbugarden: late October-early June
Road no. 258, Old Strynefjellsveg: late September–early June
Road no. 520, Sauda–Roldal: early December–mid-June
Road no. 882, Storvik–Bardines: open all year
Road no. 886, Vintervollen–Gr. Jacobselv: mid-January–late April

HIGHWAY SIGNS

International road signs are used.

DRIVING REGULATIONS

• A valid driver's license from any U.S. state or Canadian province is all that is needed to operate a car in Norway.
• If you rent a car in Norway, third-party liability insurance, required by law, is included in rental rates. Fire and auto theft coverage are also included in rental rates.
• Seat belts are compulsory for front-seat passengers and, if available, also for back-seat passengers.
• Speed limits are 50 kph/30 mph in cities and towns, 80 kph/50 mph outside built-up and populated areas of cities and towns, 90 kph/56 mph on expressways.

PARKING

Parking meters are in use in some towns. Free use of unexpired time on meters is authorized. There are three types of parking meters: yellow, one hour's parking; gray, two hours; brown, three hours.

A sign stating ALL STANS FORBUDT means that stopping or parking is prohibited.

EMERGENCY INFORMATION

Local phone numbers for the police, fire, and ambulance are found in all regional phone books.

GASOLINE STATIONS

Stations are located all over Norway. Some close overnight on weekdays, and some close on weekends. Unleaded gas is labeled *blyfri* or *blyfritt kraftstoff.*

A bridge over the Vistula River provides access to Warsaw's Old Town, in the background. (LOT Airlines)

POLAND

CAPITAL: Warsaw (Warszawa)

POPULATION: 37,000,000

AREA: 122,349 square mi/313,716 square km

CURRENCY UNIT: zloty (ZL) and groszy (GR)

LANGUAGE: Polish

TIME FROM UNITED STATES: Eastern Standard plus 6 hours

TELEPHONE ACCESS CODES: to United States, USA Direct from Warsaw, 010–480–0111 (outside Warsaw, 0010–480–0111); from United States, 48

EMBASSIES/CONSULATES: *American Embassy,* Aleje Ujazdowskie 29/31, Warsaw; phone: 283041–9. United States Consulate, Ul. Stolarska 9, Cracow; phone: 22–77–93. Ul. Chopina, Poznan; phone: 52–95–86. *British Embassy,* Aleja Roz No. 1, 00-556 Warsaw; phone: 281001–5. *United States Consulate,* Polish Consulate General, 233 Madison Avenue, New York, NY 10016; phone: (212) 889–8360. *Polish Consulate General,* 1525 North Astor Street, Chicago, IL 60610; phone: (312) 337–8166. *Consular Division of Polish Embassy,* 2224 Wyoming Avenue NW, Washington, D.C. 20006; phone: (202) 234–2501. *British Consulate, Consulate General of Polish People's Republic,* 73 New Cavendish Street, London W1; phone: (071) 636–4533. Polish Tourist Information Centre, POLORBIS Travel Ltd., 82 Mortimer Street, Regent Street, London WIN 7DE; phone: (071) 637–4971

CONTACTS FOR PRETRIP PLANNING

Automobile Clubs

Warsaw: Polski Zwiazek Motorowy, Ul. Kazimierzowska 66, 02-518, Warsaw; phone: 49–93–61 or 49–41–38

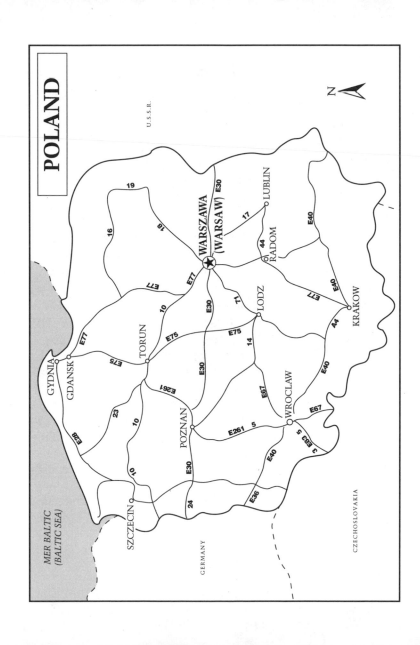

Tourist Offices

United States: Polish National Tourist Office, 333 N. Michigan Avenue, Chicago, IL 60601; phone: (312) 236–9013. ORBIS Polish Travel Bureau, 342 Madison Avenue, Suite 1512, New York, NY 10173; phone: (212) 867–5011. *Britain:* POLORBIS Travel Ltd., 82 Mortimer Street, London ViN 7DE; phone: (071) 637–49–71/3. *Poland:* ORBIS National Tourist Enterprise, Ul. Bracka 16, 00-028 Warsaw, phone: 26–02–71

Ferries

Polferries: *United States,* EuroCruises (800) 688–EURO. Routes from Gdansk to Ystad and Oxelosund in Sweden, and Helsinki.

Airlines

LOT: United States, (800) 223–0593 or (212) 869–1074; Britain, (071) 580–5037; Poland, 28–10–09, 28–75–80 or 952 (Warsaw)

TOPOGRAPHY

Poland is located in the center of the European continent. As a lowland country, Poland's average height above sea level is 562 feet. Topographic regions run in parallel strips as follows, from north to south: the Baltic coast, the Pomeranian and Masurian lakes, the central Polish lowland, the Lublin highlands, Little Poland, and the Sudete and Carpathian mountains. Driving is a fine way to enjoy the variety of terrain Poland has to offer.

The motorway system in Poland is in its incipient stages, with short sections completed west of Wroclaw, west of Krakow, and east of Poznan, but there is a long, divided four-lane highway from Warsaw to the Czech border. Main highways do link all the other important cities, and an extensive system of secondary roads blankets most of the country.

The Baltic coast is one of sandy beaches, sandbars, dunes,

bays, fishing villages, resorts, and health spas. To the northwest Wolin Island is a national park and forest preserve; this island is accessible by road. The Hel Peninsula contains the Amber Coast, where the sand sparkles with minerals and yellow sand.

The Pomeranian and Masurian lake districts lie amongst forested hills. Poland has almost, but not quite, as many lakes as Finland. Visitors come for boating, swimming, and fishing to both lakes and rivers in these areas. During the winter ice boating and skating are popular. A network of roads links the lakes in this popular touring area.

The center of the country is a lowland of wide river valleys including the Vistula, Odra, Warta, and Bug. The Bialowieska National Park, the largest European primeval forest, has some oaks that are more than 1,000 years old. UNESCO labeled the forest as

Castle Square in Warsaw retains all of its Old World charm.
(LOT Airlines)

a "World Reservation of the Biosphere." Bison, lynx, moose, tarpan ponies, foxes, deer, and wild boars also roam within the forest. Even with all of this wildlife motorists are free to drive through the park.

In the south two mountain ranges rise: the Sudety and the Carpathians. The Sudety is one of the undiscovered jewels in Poland. Take a drive to drink in mountain views in this land of spruce forests and clear mountain lakes. The highest peak in the Sudety is Mount Sniezka at 5,260 feet.

The Carpathians include the Tatras massif, very much like the Alps. Mt. Rysy, at 8,200 feet, is the highest peak there. The Western Carpathian Mountains include the Beskydy and Pieniny ranges along the Slovak border. The Eastern Carpathian Mountains include the Bieszczady Mountains with their green pastures and few people. Winter sports and hiking centers include Zakopane and Szczyrk; there is access by road.

ROAD CONDITIONS

Main roads are in good condition, but some of the secondary roads are narrow and difficult to drive with slippery or cobbled surfaces. Friends say that some Polish drivers pass indiscriminately as well as exceed the speed limit. Drivers should be aware of horse-drawn carts, especially those driven at night without lights. After a winter storm roads are cleared promptly.

HIGHWAY SIGNS

Road signs conform with the international code.

All roads in Poland are provided with a full range of road signs. Main roads are international highways designated with the letter "E."

DRIVING REGULATIONS

• The speed limit for automobiles is 60 kph/37 mph in built-up areas, 90 kph/55 mph elsewhere, and 110 kph/68 mph on expressways.
• Drive on the right, pass on the left.
• The use of seat belts is required.
• A driver's license in accordance with the international convention is required.
• The car registration card must be carried.
• The Green Card is required, or an insurance policy may be purchased at the border.

PARKING

Parking lights are compulsory on unlighted streets at night. Drivers may park with the wheels of one side of the vehicle on the pavement if the gross weight of the vehicle is less than 2,500 kg and if pedestrians are not obstructed.

Parking is prohibited 5 meters in front of a pedestrian crossing.

EMERGENCY INFORMATION

In case of accident dial 999, for police 997, and fire department 998.

GASOLINE STATIONS

Foreign travelers may buy fuel without any limits, using fuel coupons. The coupons may be purchased with foreign currency from the Polish Automobile Federation border agents and at currency-exchange counters in ORBIS hotels in Poland or in ORBIS Polish Travel Bureau in the tourist's country of residence. Unused coupons may be exchanged at any currency window, provided that they are accompanied by the receipt issued at the time of purchase.

Stations are located every 30–40 km (20–25 mi) on secondary roads. Those along international roads and in larger cities are open twenty-four hours a day. Lead-free gasoline, labeled *benzyna bezolowin,* may be purchased at selected gasoline stations.

A "barco rabelo" loaded with wine sails peacefully into the harbor of Porto. (Portuguese National Tourist Office)

PORTUGAL

CAPITAL: Lisbon (Lisboa)
POPULATION: 10,000,000
AREA: 36,007 square mi/92,326 square km
CURRENCY UNIT: escudo (ESC) and centavos
LANGUAGE: Portuguese
TIME FROM UNITED STATES: Eastern Standard plus 5 hours
TELEPHONE ACCESS CODES: to United States, 097–1; from United States, 351
EMBASSIES: *American Embassy,* Avenida das Forcas Armadas (a Sete Rios), 1600 Lisbon; phone: 726–6600 or 726–8880. *British Embassy,* 35/37 Rua de Santa Domingos, a Lapa Lisbon 1296; phone: 661191 or 661122

CONTACTS FOR PRETRIP PLANNING

Automobile Clubs

Lisbon: Automovel Club de Portugal, Rua Rosa Araujo 24-26, Apartado 2594, Lisbon P-1000; phone: 563931

Tourist Offices

United States: Portuguese National Tourist Office, 590 Fifth Avenue, New York, NY 10036-4704; phone: (212) 354–4403. *Britain:* Portuguese National Tourist Office, New Bond Street House, 1 New Bond Street, London W1Y ONP; phone: (071) 493–3873. *Portugal:* National Tourist Office, Praca dos Restauradores (Palacio Foz), Lisbon P-1000; phone: 346–33–14; Lisbon Tourist Department, R. Portas St. Antao, 141, 1100 Lisbon P-1000; phone: 372579/327935

Airlines

TAP Portugal: *United States,* (800) 221–7370; *Britain,* (071) 828–0262

TOPOGRAPHY

Portugal is the westernmost country of Europe, and its most southwesterly point, Cape St. Vincent, is the corner of the continent. Portugal offers a variety of terrain including sandy beaches, precipitous mountains, vineyards, cork forests, fishing villages, and densely wooded granite ledges. With a car visitors can enjoy several varieties of scenic splendor in a single day.

The small scale of Portugal's territory does not justify an elaborate motorway system, and there is none, apart from a few spurs leading out of Lisbon and Oporto. A glance at the road map will show you that main highways are scarce and smaller roads plentiful, indicating that covering great distances at high speed is not a priority. Some of the national highways bypass towns, but many do not. An exception is the route along the Algarve, Portugal's popular southern riviera coast, where the highway runs slightly inland of all the beach towns, with side roads leading to the water. A granite mountain range, the Serra de Monchique, lies in the northwestern section of the Algarve.

The province just north of the Algarve, the Alentejo, covers a large part of Portugal. This area is flat and supports cork trees, usually stripped of their marketable bark. Much of the land is barren and dry, its population sparse. Slow secondary roads lie in an west-east orientation; if you want to save time driving to Lisbon, choose the main road, not the scenic, meandering ones.

North of Lisbon the province of Estremadura contains coastal fishing villages on sandy beaches alternating with rocky cliffs. Cabo da Roca, a cape with a lighthouse, is identified by a sign reading WHERE THE LAND ENDS AND THE SEA BEGINS. The tip of this point is the most westerly spot of continental Europe. The Serra de Sintra range is wooded and was once volcanic. We have driven a pleasant circle route from Lisbon through Estoril, Cascais, Cabo da Roca, Sintra, Queluz and back to Lisbon. It pays to exercise caution, though, when driving the "Marginal." The section between Lisbon and Cascais is notorious for fast, careless drivers. The road between Lisbon and Sintra, which is narrow and winding, has a poor road surface and no lights in some places. Drivers tend to speed along and pass on curves, even at night.

Two-thirds of Portugal lie north of Lisbon, much of this being prime touring country unspoiled by any signs of mass tourism. The rich Tagus valley is filled with vegetable gardens, rice paddies, hillside vineyards, and olive groves. Beira Alta and Beira

Lisbon's Avenida da Liberdade boulevard features palm trees, mosaic sidewalks, and the Praca Marques de Pombal, where the marble monument commemorates the man who redesigned the city after a disasterous nineteenth-century fire. (Portuguese National Tourist Office)

Baixa are mountainous, with sparsely populated valleys. Tras-os-Montes (beyond the mountains) is a high barren plateau, while the most northern provinces, Minho and Douro, have granite hills tightly packed with vegetation. Grape vines grow in many parts of Portugal, but they are most prolific in a wide swath along the coastal areas from Lisbon northward beyond Oporto, center of the Port country. Wine festivals make fall prime time for touring this beautiful region.

ROAD CONDITIONS

Main roads are in good condition, although near the Spanish border in the Algarve, as well as in the north, many leave something to be desired. Friends report that driving is slow along the Algarve during peak season, in summer. Some of Portugal's secondary roads are also slow, but rural landscape rewards those who travel here with fine views.

Roads through the Serra da Estrela, numbered 231, 232, 338, and 339 may be closed after a heavy snowfall.

HIGHWAY SIGNS

International signs are used.

DRIVING REGULATIONS

- Drive on the right, and pass on the left. Traffic approaching from the right must be given right-of-way.
- Speed limits in built-up areas are 60 kph/37 mph, outside towns 90 kph/55 mph, and on highways the minimum speed is 50 kph/31 mph and the maximum 120 kph/75 mph.
- Pedestrians have right-of-way at zebra-striped crossings.
- Use of a triangle is obligatory in case of emergency stops.
- Insurance is obligatory.

PARKING

Parked vehicles must be left with the front of the car facing the same direction as traffic on that street.

Some towns use parking disks, which can be obtained from the police free of charge.

EMERGENCY INFORMATION

Dial 115 if you are involved in an accident. There are also orange-colored SOS call points along some roads.

GASOLINE STATIONS

Stations are located throughout Portugal. Unleaded gas is labeled *gasolina sem chumbo.*

SCOTLAND

CAPITAL: Edinburgh

POPULATION: 5,196,000

AREA: 30,721 square mi/78,772 square km

CURRENCY UNIT: Scottish pound, equal to English pound

LANGUAGES: English and Gaelic

TIME FROM UNITED STATES: Eastern Standard plus 5 hours

TELEPHONE ACCESS CODES: to United States, 010 or USA Direct (0800) 89–0011; from United States, 44

CONSULATES: *American Consulate,* 3 Regent Terrace, Edinburgh, EH75BW; phone: (031) 556–8315

CONTACTS FOR PRETRIP PLANNING

Automobile Club

The Automobile Association, Fanum House, Erskine Harbour, Erskine, Renfrewshire PA8 6AT, Scotland; phone: (041) 812–0101

Tourist Offices

United States: British Tourist Authority, 40 W. Fifty-seventh Street, New York, NY 10019; phone: (212) 581–4700. *Scotland:* Scottish Tourist Board, Ravelston Terrace, Edinburgh; phone: (031) 332–2433

Ferries

Caledonia Macbrayne Ltd.: *United States,* (800) 221–3254 or (516) 747–8880; *Britain,* (0475) 34531 for booking, 33755 for inquiries. Routes from Oban, Ullapool, and Ardrossan to the islands

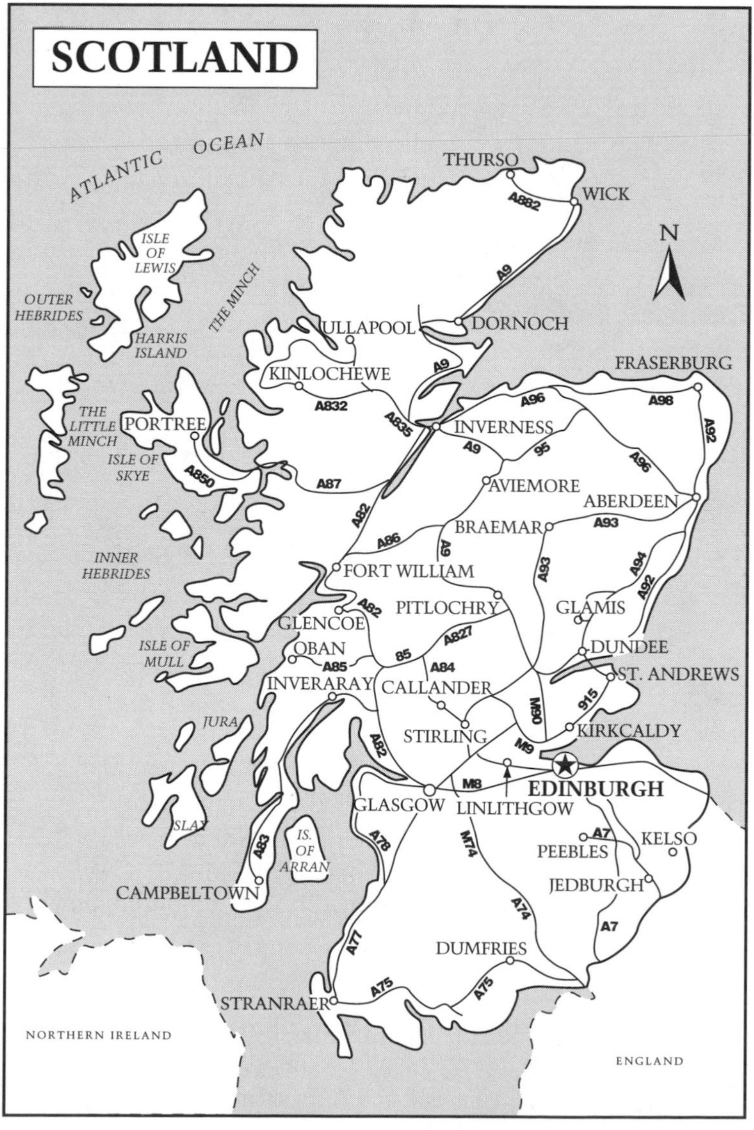

SCOTLAND

ATLANTIC OCEAN

THURSO
A882
WICK

ISLE OF LEWIS

OUTER HEBRIDES

THE MINCH

HARRIS ISLAND

A9

ULLAPOOL
DORNOCH

KINLOCHEWE

FRASERBURG

A832
A835
A9
A96
A98
A92

THE LITTLE MINCH

PORTREE
INVERNESS

ISLE OF SKYE
A850

A87
A9
95
A96

AVIEMORE
ABERDEEN

A82
A86
BRAEMAR
A93

INNER HEBRIDES

FORT WILLIAM
A9
A93
A94
A92

A82
PITLOCHRY
GLAMIS

GLENCOE
A827
DUNDEE
ST. ANDREWS

OBAN
85
A84
A85

ISLE OF MULL

INVERARAY
CALLANDER
M90
915
KIRKCALDY

JURA

A82
STIRLING
M9

ISLAY

M8
EDINBURGH

A83
GLASGOW
LINLITHGOW

IS. OF ARRAN

A78
M74
A7
KELSO

PEEBLES

CAMPBELTOWN
JEDBURGH

A77
A74
A7

DUMFRIES

A75
A75

STRANRAER

NORTHERN IRELAND

ENGLAND

N

P & O Scottish Ferries: *United States,* (800) 221–3254 or (516) 747–8880; *Britain,* (0224) 572615

Airlines

British Airways: *United States,* (800) 247–9297; *Britain,* (081) 897–4000

TOPOGRAPHY

Important regions of Scotland are so remote and isolated from each other that reaching them by car is more a necessity than a luxury. Yet the motorway system in Scotland is largely undeveloped, being restricted to a tiny urban pocket between and around Edinburgh and Glasgow. A single motorway starts south from Glasgow but becomes a dual carriageway (open-access, four-lane road) before connecting with a motorway again in Carlisle, just south of the English border. In the counties south of the Clyde and the Firth of Forth, road systems do not differ much from those in northern England, where a reasonable number of major highways is buttressed by an extensive network of secondary roads.

The same pattern holds true in lowland areas just north of the two major cities and extending as far as Stirling, Perth, Dundee, and the coastal regions around Aberdeen. Once you move into the Trossachs or the Grampian Mountains, though, only a few major roads remain, many of them running down the valleys. Beyond the Great Glen between Fort William and Inverness that almost makes northern Scotland an island, major roads almost disappear, with a single highway running up the east coast toward John o'Groats and a number of fingers stretching toward the region's many coastal lochs in the west.

In the most populous segment of Scotland, the Firth of Forth and the Clyde nearly cut the country in half on a line between its two major cities, Edinburgh and Glasgow. The Lothian Plains surround Edinburgh, while just north of Glasgow the lochs and rolling hills of the Trossachs provide one of the most attractive and accessible areas of Scotland.

West of the Clyde estuary, the long island barrier that shelters the Scottish coast from the wrath of the North Atlantic includes the Isle of Arran (take a car ferry from Ardrossan to Brodick or, in summer, drive out the Kintyre Peninsula from Inverary to the ferry at Lochranza); Mull of Kintyre; Jura (car ferry from Kintyre to Feolin), where the scenic 24-mile road ends in a dirt track; and Islay (car ferry from Kintyre to Port Ellen and Askaig).

The Highland Boundary Fault tracks northeastward from Hellensburgh on the Clyde to Stonehaven on the North Sea coast; it marks the southern edge of the highlands. It includes the dra-

Urquhart Castle, on Loch Ness, controlled the Great Glen, which cuts through Scotland from Fort William to Inverness. (Scottish Tourist Board)

matic fjords, moors, glens, and peaks of the Western Highlands—Oban, Rannoch, Glencoe, Ben Nevis. The Cairngorm Mountains fill the center of the highlands and rise to 4,000 feet, drawing hikers, climbers, and many skiers during the winter. To the east, the coastline along the Moray Firth, sometimes called the Scottish Riviera, attracts vacationers.

The Great Glen fault is the second deep slash across Scotland. Mostly covered by water, it separates the Grampian Mountains from the Northwest Highlands as it runs from Loch Linnhe through Loch Ness to the Moray Firth. From this divide northward the country remains mountainous and sparsely settled all the way to Cape Wrath and John o'Groats, and it is surrounded by eight hundred islands including the Inner and Outer Hebrides to the west and the Orkneys and Shetlands farther offshore to the north. Some of them are uninhabited and tourists bypass many more, but the Isle of Skye (five-minute car ferry from Kyle of Lochalsh to Kyleakin all year or, in summer, from Glenelg to Kylerhea) and the Isle of Mull (car ferry from Oban to Craignure) are two that drivers find easy to reach. If you have a taste for the desolate but uniquely beautiful landscape, they are well worth a visit.

ROAD CONDITIONS

Main roads are in good condition. Some secondary roads are winding and narrow in mountainous areas. Unenclosed sheep graze about almost everywhere in the highland, so be prepared to stop suddenly.

HIGHWAY SIGNS

Motorways are classified "M" and compare with U.S. interstate highways. Those marked with "M" in parentheses will eventually be motorways. Primary roads are marked "A" and are like U.S.

multilane and some divided highways. Other roads are marked "B."

DRIVING REGULATIONS

- Drive on the left in Scotland, as in England.
- Speed on the motorways and dual carriageways (two-lane roads) is 70 mph, other roads 60 mph and in built-up areas 30 mph.
- Seat-belt use is compulsory.
- Pedestrians have the right-of-way when they are on the black-and-white zebra crossings. In the area marked by zigzag lines on the approach to a zebra crossing, you must not pass. At pelican crossings (crossings operated by pedestrians who push a button to change stop and go signals for motorists) the signals have the same meaning as traffic lights, except that a flashing amber signal will follow the red stop signal. When the amber light is flashing, you must yield way to any pedestrians on the crossing.

PARKING

Drivers may not park within the area marked by zigzag lines on either side of a zebra-striped crossing nor in the zone indicated by rows of studs on the approach to pelican crossings.

Parking disks or tickets obtained from a machine in the parking area are necessary along most streets and in parking lots.

EMERGENCY INFORMATION

The national emergency telephone number is 999 to reach police, fire brigade, and medical service.

GASOLINE STATIONS

There are petrol stations throughout Scotland. We still recommend filling up before you cross mountainous areas in the Highlands. (We remember our anxiety in the fifties as we coasted down hills with a low gas tank.) Many stations now sell unleaded petrol at green pumps marked "unleaded BS7070 premium."

Designed by Antonio Gaudi, the Temple of the Holy Family, in Barcelona, was left unfinished after his death. (Tourist Office of Spain)

SPAIN

CAPITAL: Madrid

POPULATION: 39,000,000

AREA: 196,753 square mi/504,496 square km

CURRENCY UNIT: Spanish peseta

LANGUAGE: Spanish

TIME FROM UNITED STATES: Eastern Standard plus 6 hours

TELEPHONE ACCESS CODES: to United States, 07; from United States, 34

EMBASSIES: *American Embassy,* Serrano 75, Madrid; phone: 276–3400 or 3600. *British Embassy,* Calle de Fernando el Santo 16, Madrid 4; phone: 419–02–00

CONTACTS FOR PRETRIP PLANNING

Automobile Clubs

Madrid: Real Automovil Club de Espana, Gen. Sanjurjo no. 10, E-Madrid 3; phone: 447–32–00

Tourist Offices

United States: National Tourist Office of Spain, 666 Fifth Avenue, New York, NY 10022; phone: (212) 759–8822. *Britain:* National Tourist Office of Spain, 57/58 St. James's Street, London SW1A 1LD; phone: (071) 499–0901. *Spain:* Madrid Tourist Office, Torre de Madrid, Plaza de Espana; phone: (91) 241–2325

Ferries

Brittany Ferries: *United States, (*800) 221–3254 or (516) 747–8880; *Britain,* Portsmouth (0705) 827701, and Plymouth (0752) 221–321

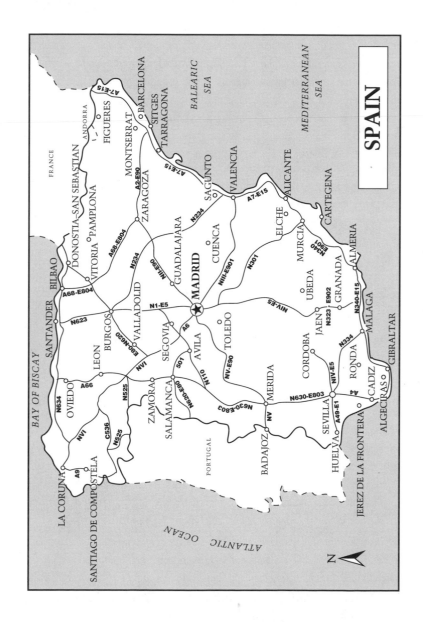

Airlines

Iberia: *United States,* (800) 221–9741; *Britain,* (071) 437–5622

TOPOGRAPHY

Spain is one of the most mountainous countries in Europe. Sierras (serrated ranges) march all around the borders and coastlines. Since Spain is a peninsula with a sunny climate, its resort coastlines along the Mediterranean, Atlantic, and Bay of Biscay are extensive, each having an enticing name familiar to many sunseekers. One January we chose to drive all around Spain's coasts and its border with Portugal, with dips inland to the Sierras and the Meseta. We were amazed at the variety of topography along our circuit.

Spain's highway system is hard to describe because it lacks consistency, and you may be surprised by a slow route between major cities or an unusually fast ride through deserted territory. The greatest motorway development does not link everything to Madrid, as one might expect, where spurs of *autopista* lead outward and then stop abruptly. (Madrid is, however, the hub of national roads leading outward in all directions.) The long motorway sections appear in the northeast, where one east-west autopista connects Barcelona with Zaragoza, Burgos, and Bilbao, and another runs along the Mediterranean coast from the French border as far south as Alicante. (Once, having arrived at Alicante, we were determined to reach Cartagena. We followed the main route to Elche and Murcia; then, at a crawl, we crested the pass over the Sierra de Carroscoy. It was a surprise to find a city at the end of such a desolate, poor road.) There are further autopista connectors in the southwest from Seville to Huelva and to Cadiz, but no integrated autopista system as yet.

National roads connect major cities, but each one has its own character—determined more by the terrain and other circumstances than its classification. The coastal road through posh resorts along the Costa del Sol is overused and underdeveloped, and the main road from Madrid to the ferry port of Santander is jammed with heavy truck traffic between Spain and England. But in spite of all these anomalies, the road system works, and you will soon learn which routes to avoid and which to prefer. Within the less congested regions that you will want to tour, almost any road will lead you into countryside worth seeing.

The northern provinces—Galicia, Asturias, Cantabria, and Navarre—are known as "Wet Spain" because of their humid climate. This is Basque country, mountainous and beautiful but with few primary roads. Car ferries leave Santander for England year-round. Yet one January we almost didn't make it because a blizzard forced trucks to slip and grind up the two-lane road from central Spain. We learned to zip past them in our trusty Saab and made the ferry with minutes to spare, even after one flat tire made us empty the trunk in pouring rain to reach the spare "toy" tire.

Just down the east coast from France and the Pyrenees, the Costa Brava is noted for its wild craggy cliffs with pine trees that somehow survive overhanging the sea. Inland from Barcelona a sawtoothed mountain range can be seen from miles away; Monserrat is one of the mountains in the range. Drive to the base of the cable car for the last leg up the mountain to the monastery.

Along the eastern shore, the Costa Dorada, Costa del Ahazar, and the Costa Blanca are lined with holiday apartments interspersed with fishing and ferry ports. The Costa del Sol stretches from the coastal turning at Almeria all the way to Gibraltar. It appeals to vacationers who either want the rugged mountains overlooking beaches to be found in the east or the low, sandy beaches in the western sector. Subtropical vegetation brings color to that beautiful but sometimes overcrowded coast; driving can be slow behind too many sun-seekers.

A short distance inland from the Costa del Sol, the Sierra Nevada Mountains appeal to skiers, who can split a day between the slopes and the city or the beaches. A short but wonderful road takes you from the lushness of Granada to the barren austerity of the highest mountains in the country, where the ski resort is appropriately named "Solynieve" (sun and snow); reaching more than 10,000 feet, these mountains hold snow from November to May. However, the roads up into the Sierra Nevadas are kept clear all year round, and we did not need chains even in January.

Farther west, Cordoba, Seville, and the seaport Cadiz all lie in the flood plain of the Guadalquivir, a river with variable flow from the dry interior of Spain. The Mesata in the center of Spain is a large, flat, and high plateau surrounded by mountains. "Dry Spain" is so called because of its very sparse water, brown hues, and barren spaces. In the center is Madrid, where, as in most large cities, it pays to park your car and walk or take public transportation. You will make full use of it as you move outward from the center to a circle of surrounding destinations nearby—El Escorial, Avila, Segovia, Guadalajara, and Toledo.

ROAD CONDITIONS

Motorway sections are open in some areas, and most national roads are in good condition, with a concrete surface. Some are overcrowded and a few demand extreme caution, particularly sections of the N 340 along the Costa del Sol. Secondary roads, especially in the southeastern region, are unequal in quality and require a great deal of patience to drive.

Information on passes:

Alcolea Del Pinar: 1,199 meters in height, Route N11 Guadalajara to Calatayud, usually open in winter

Alto De Las Portilla: 1,274 meters, Route 615 Palencia to Riano, usually open

Arrebatacapas: 1,220 meters, Route AV503 Avila to Cebreros, intermittent closure

Azpiroz: 616 meters, Route N240 Pamplona to San Sebastian, usually open

Barazar: 604 meters, Route N240 Vitoria to Bilbao, open

Bonaigua: 2,072 meters, Route C142 Esterri de Aneo to Viella, closed October–May

Bruch: 619 meters, Route N11 Lerida to Barcelona, open

Cabrejas: 1,150 meters, Route N400 Toledo to Cuenca, intermittent closure

Canda: 1,262 meters, Route N525 Zamora to Orense, unreliable in winter

Carrales: 1,020 meters, Route N623 Barcelonnette to Nice, closed November–mid-June

Contreras: 890 meters, Route N111 Tarancon to Requena, open

Despenaperros: 700 meters, Route NIV Valdepenas to Bailen, open

The Pabellon Plateresco palace and its ornamental pool enhance the landscape of Seville. (Tourist Office of Spain)

Escudo: 1,011 meters, Route N623 Burgos to Santander, intermittent closure

Guadarrama: 1,511 meters, Route NV1 Madrid to La Coruna, intermittent closure

Gudina: 1,262 meters, Route N525 Zamora to Orense, intermittent closure

Ibaneta: 1,057 meters, Route C135 St.-Jean-Pied-de-Port to Pamplona, usually open

Leitariegos: 1,525 meters, Route 631 Ponterrada to La Espina, intermittent closure

Lizarraga: 1,031 meters, Route N111 Logrono to San Sebastian, open

Navacerrada: 1,860 meters, Route N601 Madrid to Segovia, intermittent closure

Pourtalet: 1,794 meters, Routes N134/C136 Pau to Huesca, closed November–early June

Somport: 1,640 meters, Routes N330/N134 Pau to Zaragoza, intermittent closure

Tosas: 1,800 meters, Route N152 Barcelona to Puigcerda, usually open

HIGHWAY SIGNS

International road signs are used in Spain. In addition, you will see some blue signs, with the symbol of a camera, for example, indicating a view. A white or yellow triangle on a square warns caution.

DRIVING REGULATIONS

• Visitors need either an International Driving License or a translation of the license from home.

- Insurance requirements include the Green Card with third-party insurance.
- A bail bond (in Spanish) is *strongly* recommended to prevent detention in case of serious accident.
- Drive on the right, pass on the left. Drivers must yield to vehicles coming from the right.
- Drivers entering a main road must yield to vehicles moving in both directions.
- In built-up areas the speed limit is 60 kph/37 mph. Outside built-up areas the speed limit on motorways is 120 kph/74 mph, on roads with more than one lane in each direction 100 kph/62 mph, and on other roads 90 kph/56 mph.
- Where visibility is limited at an intersection, drivers must not drive more than 50 kph/31 mph.
- Seat belts are mandatory. Children under fourteen years may not ride in the front seat.
- Every vehicle must have a set of spare bulbs.
- When a driver behind signals an intention to pass, the other driver must flick the right-hand signal to demonstrate understanding.
- A warning triangle is compulsory.

PARKING

Parking disks are used in blue zones. Parking is not allowed within 5 meters of corners, crossroads, fork-roads, and entrances to public buildings. On one-way streets vehicles must park on uneven house-numbered sides on uneven days and vice versa.

EMERGENCY INFORMATION

In an emergency in Madrid and Barcelona, dial 091 for police, 092 for medical help, and 2323232 for the fire department. In other places dial 003 for the operator.

GASOLINE STATIONS

You can find stations throughout Spain except in desolate areas.
It is always wise to run on the top half of a tank. Unleaded gasoline is labeled *sin plomo*.

Gotaplatsen, in Göteborg, contains the "Poseidon Fountain" by Carl Milles. (Swedish National Tourist Office)

SWEDEN

CAPITAL: Stockholm

POPULATION: 8,000,000

AREA: 175,486 square mi/449,964 square km

CURRENCY UNIT: Swedish krona and ore

LANGUAGE: Swedish

TIME FROM UNITED STATES: Eastern Standard plus 6 hours

TELEPHONE ACCESS CODES: to United States, 009 or USA Direct, 020–795–611; from United States, 46

EMBASSIES: *American Embassy,* Strandvagen 101, S-115 27 Stockholm; phone: (08) 783–5300. *British Embassy,* Skarpogatan 6-8, S-115 27 Stockholm; phone: (08) 66–701–40

CONTACTS FOR PRETRIP PLANNING

Automobile Clubs

Stockholm: M-Motormannens Riksforbund, Box 5855, S-102 48, Stockholm; phone: (08) 782–38–00. Swedish Touring Club, Vasagatan 48, Box 25, S-101 20 Stockholm; phone: (08) 790–31

Tourist Offices

United States: Swedish Tourist Board, 655 Third Avenue, New York, NY 10017; phone: (212) 949–2333. *Britain:* Swedish Tourist Board, 29-31 Oxford Street, London W1R 1RE; phone: (071) 437–5816. *Sweden:* Sveriges Turistrad, Box 7473, S-103 92 Stockholm; phone: (08) 789–20–00

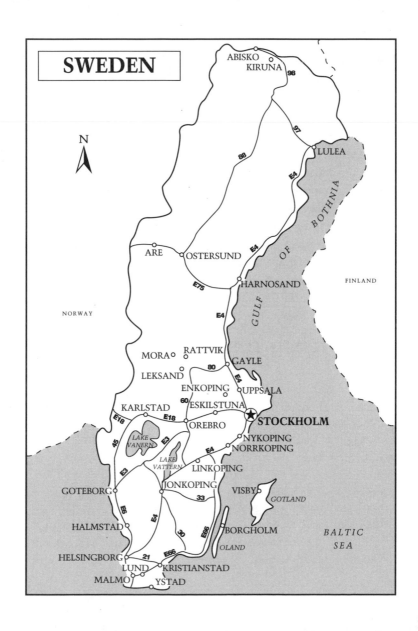

Ferries

Gotland Line: *United States,* EuroCruises (800) 668–EURO.
Routes from Nynasham to Visby, Gotland

Polferries: *United States,* EuroCruises (800) 668–EURO. Route
from Oxelsund (near Stockholm); Ystad to Gdansk and
Swinovjscie, Poland

Scandinavian Seaways: *United States,* EuroCruises (800)
668–EURO; DFDS (800) 533–3755 or (305) 491–7909; *Britain,*
(0255) 241–234 or 240–240; *Sweden:* 042–128–100. Routes from
Göteborg to Harwich and Newcastle; Oskarshamn to Visby;
Stockholm to Turku, Helsinki, and Tallinn

Sealink Stena Line: *Britain,* (0233) 646–801

Viking Line: *United States,* EuroCruises (800) 668–EURO. Routes
from Stockholm to Helsinki, Leningrad, Estonia, and Turku

Wasa Line: *United States,* EuroCruises (800) 668–EURO. Routes
from Sundsvall to Finland

Airlines

SAS: *United States,* (800) 221–2350; *Britain,* (071) 734–4020

TOPOGRAPHY

As in Finland and Norway, most of Sweden's small population
lives in the southern quarter of a very large country, and the road
system reflects that concentration. Apart from the centers of a
few cities, no part of Sweden is densely populated; just east of the
Stockholm city limits lies an archipelago of rocky, wooded islands. Yet, in spite of a small population and vast stretches of
land, Sweden's highway system is very good and improving—a
state of affairs perhaps not surprising for a country that manufac-
tures Saabs and Volvos.

The highway system is short on motorways, which now exist
only in segments of a great triangle linking Malmo with Göteborg

on the west coast and Stockholm on the east. In addition to these connections between Sweden's three major cities, the first pieces of a major motorway between Stockholm and Oslo are in service, but the route is far from complete. For the present southern Sweden has a first-rate system of primary highways. Some that are labeled secondary, like the road from Halmstad to Jonkoping, for example, would be counted as national roads in many European countries. The number of major highways diminishes as one moves north of the Stockholm-Oslo line, but two lead north almost as far as Sweden goes, and they are crossed by arteries from Trondheim and Mo-i-Rana in Norway.

The topography of Sweden can be described as one big slide, because the land slopes toward the south and east from the

The Zorn House at Mora in Dalarna was once the home of the great Swedish painter and sculptor Anders Zorn. (Swedish National Tourist Office)

mountains along the Norwegian border. Northern Sweden (Norrland), richly loaded with mountains, lakes and rivers, is popular with hikers, climbers, skiers, and fishermen. Many Swedes have remote vacation huts, and resorts offer activity both winter and summer. A network of roads serves this region.

Central Sweden (Svealand) includes Stockholm, the "Venice of the North," which was created on fourteen islands. The idyllic archipelago east of the city clusters green islands with red houses against a backdrop of blue sea. Residents of Stockholm use the archipelago as their playground. Visitors can drive onto the edges of the archipelago or take cruises out to the islands. Northwest of Stockholm, Lake Siljan lies in the midst of the woods and rolling hills of Dalarna. Large lakes in the center of the country (Gotaland) include Vanern and Vattern, set in a wooded landscape that reminds us very much of our native Minnesota.

Southern Sweden is filled with rolling hills and fertile farmland. The province of Skane has beaches and major ports, including Malmo; it once had lots of timber but now contains a mixture of fields and forests. A string of low hills stretches southeast across Skane from the headlands of Cape Kullen, just north of Helsingborg. The long low islands of Oland and Gotland lie off the east coast. A causeway and bridge from Kalman provide easy access to Oland by car. Car ferry service is available all year to Visby in Gotland from Oskarshamn and Nynashamn. During the summer ferries sail from Stockholm, Vastervik or Grankullavik on Oland to Visby.

ROAD CONDITIONS

Roads are in good condition in the south; some in the north are gravel. On major highways, a climbing lane enables drivers to move past slower vehicles. Although most two-lane roads are in good condition, there are often no shoulders.

HIGHWAY SIGNS

European network major roads are indicated by white-on-green signs. National roads have white on blue. Most roads have signs with a number and a name. Most road signs conform to those in the international code.

DRIVING REGULATIONS

• Speed limits are indicated by road signs on all roads. They are 110, 90, or 70 kph (69, 56, 43 mph) outside urban areas and 50 kph/31 mph in cities and towns. Slower speed limits are posted in some areas. Expressway speeds are 110 kph/69 mph. There is rigid obedience to speed limits.

• A valid driver's license from any American state or Canadian province is accepted.

• Seat belts are required of all passengers.

• Drive on the right, pass on the left. Traffic from the right has right-of-way. This rule also applies in principle at traffic circles; most, however, are controlled by signs giving right-of-way to vehicles on the circle (that is, to vehicles coming from the left).

• When a driver gives warning of an intention to pass, an answering signal should be given.

• Headlights must be on whenever a car is in motion, day or night.

PARKING

Parking regulations follow international usage.

A circular sign with a red St. Andrew's cross on a blue background, surrounded by a red border, prohibits parking.

Parking meters are in use.

Parked vehicles on a dimly lit road at night must keep parking lights on.

EMERGENCY INFORMATION

The emergency number in Sweden is 90000, which should be used only in case of accidents. Motorists who break down on the road should call the local number of Larmtjanst, an organization that provides twenty-four-hour service nationwide.

GASOLINE STATIONS

There are stations all over the country, but outside of large towns they do not stay open at night. In the North stations may be located far apart. There are some self-service stations on main roads. Unleaded gasoline is labeled *blyfri*.

Engelberg, central Switzerland's premiere resort, features a twelfth-century Benedictine abbey as well as a cable car to the summit (10,627 feet) of Titlis, the region's highest peak. (Swiss National Tourist Office)

SWITZERLAND

CAPITAL: Bern

POPULATION: 6,566,800

AREA: 16,104 square mi/41,293 square km

CURRENCY UNIT: Swiss franc

LANGUAGES: German, French, Italian, and Romansh

TIME FROM UNITED STATES: Eastern standard plus 6 hours

TELEPHONE ACCESS CODES: to United States, 001 or USA Direct, 046–05–0011; from United States, 41

EMBASSIES: *American Embassy,* Jubilaeumstrasse 93, 3005 Bern; phone: (031) 437011. *British Embassy,* Thunstrasse 50, 3005 Bern; phone: (031) 44–50–21/6

CONTACTS FOR PRETRIP PLANNING

Automobile Clubs

Geneva: Touring Club Suisse (TCS), rue Pierre-Fatio 9, 1211 Geneva; phone: (022) 737–12–12. Basel: TCS, Steinentorstrasse 13, 4051 Basel; phone: (061) 23–19–56. *Bern:* TCS, Thunstrasse 63, 3006 Bern; phone: (031) 44–22–22. *Lausanne:* TCS, Avenue Juste-Olivier 10-12, 1006 Lausanne; phone: (021) 20–20–11. *Lucerne:* TCS, Burgerstrasse 22, 6003 Lucerne; phone: (041) 23–21–23. *Zurich:* TCS, Alfred-Escher-Strasse 38, 8002 Zurich; phone: (01) 202–65–50

Tourist Offices

United States: Swiss National Tourist Office, 608 Fifth Avenue, New York, NY 10020; phone: (212) 757–5944. *Britain:* Swiss National Tourist Office, Swiss Centre, New Coventry Street, London W1V 8EE; phone: (071) 734–1921

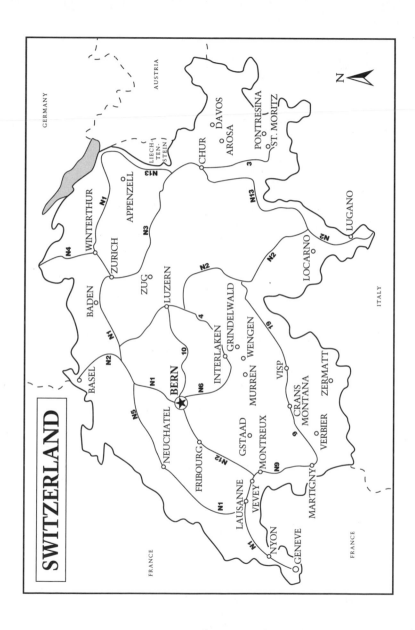

Airlines

Swissair: *United States,* (800) 221–4750, (718) 995– 8400(New York), (312) 641–8830 (Chicago); *Britain,* (071) 439–4144

TOPOGRAPHY

Swiss maps are among the best in the world, and even a cursory glance at the tourist map of the home cantons will give you an inkling about the highway system, which is simply first-rate. The major cities of Switzerland, all lying in a string just north of the Alps, are connected by motorways, which you may call autoroutes, autobahns, or autostradas in the three language areas of Switzerland. By any name they're good, and they extend in each direction to France, Germany, Austria, and Italy. Apart from the motorways, almost every valley has a good paved road, and secondary roads climb the mountain walls as far as common sense dictates. Foreign drivers in Switzerland complain about only one thing—the road tax levied on all entering vehicles—but they are getting what they pay for.

Motorists will find it easy to plan any number of circle routes by car in Switzerland, such as the lake area in the northeast and center, the Grisons in the southeast, Bernese Oberland and Valais in the south, Lake Geneva in the southwest, and the Jura heading from southwest to northwest.

Eastern Switzerland borders Germany, Austria, and Liechtenstein. To the north Lake Constance provides shimmering beauty, as well as Lake Zurich and Lake Lucerne. The Rhine River leads down into the Grisons and the Alps. Farther south ski resorts nestle in the mountains; all are easily accessible by car with some switchback roads thrown in for interest.

Moving along to the area that borders Italy, visitors find a more Mediterranean climate. Lake Maggiore extends its long finger up to Locarno and Lake Como to Lugano. The roads around both lakes are spectacular but can be slow if you're in a hurry.

Still farther west lies the Rhone River valley, the Jungfrau, the Matterhorn, and finally the expanses of Lake Geneva.

Central Switzerland has its charms as part of the Mittelland, or central plateau. Here hills, ravines, and valleys are interspersed with lakes. And to the northwest the Jura Mountains form the last stubborn barrier that protects this magic mountain world from intrusion.

ROAD CONDITIONS

It cannot be easy to keep roads well maintained in such a mountainous country, but the Swiss continue to do a great job. Swift action is taken during and after a storm. We'd like to see any flatter country whip into action so fast—our own southern United States included. Touring Club Suisse in Geneva, (022) 35–80–00, gives current conditions on mountain passes. Information is also available in French, German, and Italian by dialing 162 (weather) and 163 (roads). Watch for signs saying *chaines à neige obligatoires* (snow chains compulsory).

Information on mountain passes:

Albula: 2,312 meters, Tiefencastel to La Punt, closed November–mid-May

Bernina: 2,323 meters, Pontresina to Poschiavo, open all year

Brunig: 1,007 meters, Meiringen to Sachseln, open all year

Col des Mosses: 1,445 meters, Aigle to Chateau-d'Oex, open all year

Col du Pillon: 1,546 meters, Aigle to Gsteig, open all year

Fluela: 2,383 meters, Davos to Susch, open all year

Forclaz: 1,527 meters, Martigny to Chamonix, open all year

Furka: 2,431 meters, Gletsch to Andermatt, closed November–May

Great St. Bernard: 2,469 meters, Thusis to Bellinzona, closed November–June except through tunnel

Grimsel: 2,165 meters, Meiringen to Gletsch, closed late October–early June

Jaun: 1,509 meters, Bulle to Boltigen, closed October–mid-April

Julier: 2,284 meters, Tiefencastel to Silvaplana, open all year

Klausen: 1,948 meters, Altdorf to Linthal, November–early June

Lukmanier: 1,916 meters, Disentis to Biasca, closed November–May

Maloja: 1,815 meters, Chiavenna to Silvaplana, open all year

Nufenen: 2,478 meters, Airolo to Ulrichen, closed late October–early June

Oberalp: 2,045 meters, Andermatt to Disentis, closed late November–June

Ofen: 2,149 meters, Route 28 Zernez to Santa Maria, open all year

St. Gotthard: 2,108 meters, Andermatt to Airolo, closed October–May

San Bernardino: 2,065 meters, Thusis to Bellinzona, closed November–late May

Simplon: 2,005 meters, Brig to Domodossola, open all year; there is a rail tunnel from Brig to Iselle

Splugen: 2,113 meters, Thusis to Chiavenna, closed November–May

Susten: 2,224 meters, Innertkirchen to Wassen, closed late October–mid-June

Umbrail: 2,501 meters, Santa Maria to Stelvio, closed late October–mid-June

HIGHWAY SIGNS

Most signs follow the international code.

DRIVING REGULATIONS

• Speed limits on superhighways are 120 kph/75 mph, other roads 80 kph/50 mph, and in towns 50 kph/31 mph.

• Driver's licenses of Western Hemisphere countries are accepted.

• Minimum driving age is eighteen years. Car rental companies reserve the right, however, to set their own age limits, which are generally higher.

• Drive on the right, pass on the left. Vehicles coming from the right have right-of-way.

• Seat belts must be worn while driving. Children under twelve must not be seated in the front seats.

• Dimmed headlights must be used while driving through road tunnels.

• An annual road toll, the Vignette, is levied on all cars and motorcycles. Permits are available at border crossings, as well as at any Swiss post office, and are valid for multiple reentry into Switzerland within the duration of the licensed period (one calendar year).

• When chains are prescribed, they must be fitted on two drive wheels.

PARKING

Motorists with a parking disk may park in blue zones. Disks can be obtained from the police, service stations, kiosks, and restaurants.

EMERGENCY INFORMATION

In case of emergency call 117 for police and ambulance, 118 for fire, and 140 for "Touring Secours," which is a breakdown service. Dial 163 for road conditions.

GASOLINE STATIONS

Stations are usually open 8:00 A.M.–10:00 P.M. After these hours gasoline is available from self-service stations using bills of SFR 10 and 20. Unleaded gasoline is labeled *sans plomb* or *bleifrei* or *senza piombo.*

Istanbul's Galata Bridge crosses Golden Horn, focal point of the city's daily life. (Turkish Culture and Information Office)

TURKEY

CAPITAL: Ankara

POPULATION: 55,000,000

AREA: 304,200 square mi/780,000 square km

CURRENCY UNIT: Turkish lira (TL)

LANGUAGE: Turkish

TIME FROM UNITED STATES: Eastern Standard plus 7 hours

TELEPHONE ACCESS CODES: to United States, 091 (quick-service long-distance operator); from United States, 90

EMBASSIES/CONSULATES: *American Embassy,* Ataturk Boulevard 11, Cankaya, Ankara; phone: 126–54–70. *American Consulate,* Mesrutiyet Caddesi 34, Tepebasi, Istanbul; phone: 143–62–00 or 143–62–09. Ataturk Caddesi 92, Izmir; phone: 131369 or 149426. *British Embassy,* Sehit Ersan Caddesi 46/A, Cankaya, Ankara; phone: 27–43–10/14

CONTACTS FOR PRETRIP PLANNING

Automobile Clubs

Istanbul: Turkiye Turing ve Otomobil Kurumu (TTOK), Merkez, Sisli Halaskargazi Cd. 364, Istanbul; phone: 131–46–31. *Ankara:* TTOK, Yenisehir, Adakale Sk 4/1 Ankara; phone: 13176–48–49

TTOK, Alsancak, Ataturk Bul. 370 Izmir; phone: 21–71–49

Tourist Offices

United States: Turkish General Consulate Information Office, 821 United Nations Plaza, New York, NY 10017; phone: (212) 687–2194. *Britain:* 170–173 Piccadilly, London WIV 9DD; phone: (071) 734–8681

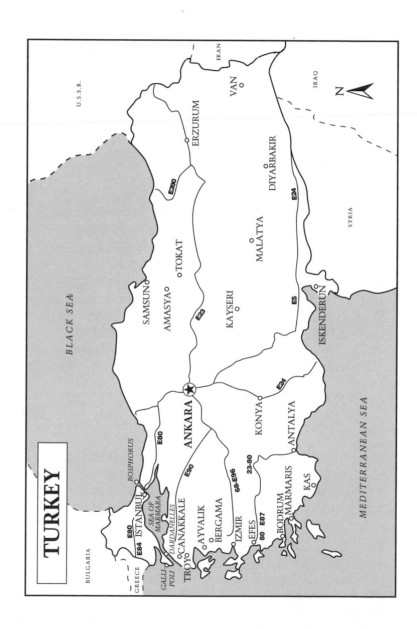

Turkey: Gazi Mustafa Kemal Bul, 33 Demirtepe, Ankara; phone: 2317380/95 or free-phone: 9.00.44.70.90. 12 Eylul Meydani, Bodrum; phone: 1091. Lskele Mey 67, Canakkale; phone: 1187. Ataturk Mah, Focaa Girisi, 1; phone: 1222. Taksim, Hilton Oteli Girisi, Istanbul; phone: 133–05–92. Ataturk Caddesi 418, Izmir; phone: 220207/8 or 224409. Cumhuriyet Meydani, Kas; phone: 1238. Ataturk Mah. Agora Carsisi, 35, Selcuk; phone: 1945–1328

Ferries

Marlines: *United States,* (800) 221–3254 or (516) 747–8880; Turkish Maritime Lines: *Istanbul,* 144–02–07/149–92–71–78

Airlines

Turkish Airlines: *United States,* (212) 986–5050–51 or (800) 874–8875; *Britain,* (071) 499/9240/47/48

TOPOGRAPHY

For drivers accustomed to the small scale of many European countries, Turkey looms large, with quite diverse topographical regions separated by generous distances. Its terrain includes snowcapped mountain peaks, valleys with a landscape resembling the moon, wide rivers surrounded by fertile agricultural land, white sandy beaches, mountainous coasts, rain forests, and rolling plains.

Turkey's motorway system is quite sparse, limited mostly to the regions surrounding major cities like Ankara, Istanbul, Izmir, and Konya. But the network of two-lane highways designated as "long-distance traffic roads" is relatively complete, considering the mountainous terrain of much of the country. These roads link all major cities and completely encircle Turkey's coasts on the Sea of Marmara, the Aegean, and the Mediterranean; one also extends along the eastern part of the Black Sea coast. In between the highways, secondary roads do the best they can, but there are still many blank spots on Turkey's road map where villages are served by roads variously designated as "roads without surface," "earth roads usable only during dry periods," and "cart tracks and footpaths."

The most important single feature of Turkey's geography is the chain of historically important waterways that separate Europe from Asia and connect the Aegean Sea with the Black Sea. At the

Visitors walk the Arcadian Way toward the Library at Ephesus.
(Turkish Culture and Information Office)

western end the peninsula of Gelibolou, site of the battle of Gallipoli during the First World War, extends out into the Aegean Sea on the European side. There the narrow Dardanelles lead from the Aegean past Canakkale into the oval-shaped Sea of Marmara, which is completely landlocked apart from its narrow connections with large seas at either end. Istanbul lies at the eastern end of the Sea of Marmara just where the famed Bosporus, now crossed by an imposing suspension bridge, separates two continents.

Toward the west from Istanbul lies eastern Thrace, which is in European Turkey. Although it is easy to drive there from Istanbul, most tourists head directly for Asian Turkey, passing south of the Sea of Marmara. But if you want to see the historically interesting Gelibolou or visit ancient Troy, it makes equal sense to take the route along the north coast of the sea and cross the Dardanelles by ferry at Canakkale.

The topography of Aegean Turkey is largely maritime, stretching from the Bosporus and the Sea of Marmara through the Dardanelles, then curving southward along the Anatolian coast as far as Kas. It includes modern ports like Istanbul and Izmir, Troy, Ephesus, and other important cities of the ancient world, and major river valleys. This is territory for package bus tours, but many visitors prefer driving from one ancient site to another on their own schedule, as many such sites are located out in the country, away from public transport.

Much of the southern Mediterranean coast is mountainous with little beach between Fethiye and Antalya and also south of Alanya. The Taurus Mountains loom from Antalya to Adana. Driving is not possible within that area unless one takes the only road from Adana to the sea and back. A very primitive road connects towns to the east from Karatas.

In the north, Cappadocia is the region between Ankara and Malatya, the Taurus Mountains and the Black Sea. The Goreme Valley near Urgup contains caves in pyramid-shaped rocks—and one can drive through this extraordinary lunar landscape.

ROAD CONDITIONS

Highways are in good condition and do not seem to be over-crowded. There is traffic in large cities, but Istanbul has a bypass. The Istanbul–Ankara highway has heavy traffic. Some of the roads in agricultural regions are shared with domestic animals that are not in a hurry to go anywhere. In remote regions it is unwise to assume that paved roads will take you anywhere you want to go.

HIGHWAY SIGNS

Turkish road signs conform to the International Protocol on Road Signs. Archaeological and historical sites are indicated by yellow signposts.

DRIVING REGULATIONS

- Drive on the right, and pass on the left.
- Carry a valid driver's license from your home state.
- Your car will be entered as imported goods on your passport and must be driven out of Turkey by a specified time.
- Two warning triangles must be carried.
- The speed limit in built-up areas is 50 kph/31 mph, outside built-up areas including motorways 90 kph/56 mph.

PARKING

A sign, PARK YAPILMAZ, indicates where parking is not allowed. Do not park on pedestrian crossings, near garage entrances, on tram or streetcar tracks, near intersections, or within 25 meters of danger signs.

GASOLINE STATIONS

Stations are located on main highways, and some of them are open twenty-four hours.

Minarets overlook the Bas Carsija quarter in Sarajevo.
(Yugoslavia National Tourist Board)

YUGOSLAVIA

Capital: Belgrade (Beograd)
Population: 23,580,000
Area: 99,764 square mi/255,804 square km
Currency unit: dinar (YD) and para
Language: Serbo-Croatian, Slovenian, and Macedonian
Time from United States: Eastern Standard plus 6 hours
Telephone access codes: to United States, 991; from United
 States, 38
Embassies: *American Embassy,* Kneza Milosa 50, Belgrade;
 phone: (011) 645–655. *British Embassy,* Generala Zdanova 46,
 Belgrade; phone: 645055/645034

CONTACTS FOR PRETRIP PLANNING

Automobile Clubs

Belgrade: Auto-Moto-Savez Jugoslavije, Ruzveltova 18, B.P. 66 YU
 11000, Belgrade; phone: (011) 401–699

Tourist Offices

United States: Yugoslav National Tourist Office, 630 Fifth Avenue,
 New York, NY 10020; phone: (212) 757–2801. *Britain:* Yugoslav
 National Tourist Office, 143 Regent Street, London W1R 8AE;
 phone: (017) 734–5243. *Yugoslavia:* Placa 1, Dubrovnik; phone:
 263–54 or 55; Terazija Street, Belgrade; phone: 635–343 or 622

Ferries

Adriatica: *United States,* (813) 394–3384; *Britain,* c/o Sealink

Stena Line: (071) 828–8947 or 1940. Routes from Dubrovnik to
Bari or Ancona; Zadar to Venice; Split to Pescara, Venice, Bari

Jadrolinija: *United States,* (800) 221–3254 or (516) 747–8880;
Britain, c/o Viamare Travel, phone: (081) 452–8231, or Yugo-
tours (071) 734–7321. Routes from Zadar and Split to Ancona,
Italy; Dubrovnik to Bari; Dubrovnik, Split, and Rijeka to Patras,
Corfu, and Igoumenitsa

Airlines

JAT Yugoslavia Airlines: *United States,* (800) 752–6528; *Britain,*
(800) 282726 or (071) 493–9399 or (071) 409–1544 for fare quotes

**[Authors' Note: Gradually for the past few years, and vio-
lently as this book is going to press, the political unity
holding Yugoslavia's republics together has disintegrated.
Whatever form of political organization evolves, we hope
that the peoples of the six republics will again welcome
tourists, as they have so generously in previous years.]**

TOPOGRAPHY

Yugoslavia is extremely mountainous—in fact, three-quarters of
the land is either mountain or highland. River valleys, including
the Danube and the Sava, and about three hundred lakes account
for the remainder of this beautiful country. But the dominant feature is even more striking: The Dinaric Mountains form a solid
wall between the interior and the Adriatic, a wall broken only by a
few passes and the Neretva River valley. Apart from the geopoliti-
cal consequences of this barrier, which are considerable, it
severely limits your ability to drive inland from the Adriatic coast
and should play an important part in planning a tour of Yugoslavia.

Of the few stretches of motorway in Yugoslavia, most are in
the north, connecting Lubljana with Trieste and Austria; around

Zagreb, heading both west and south toward Belgrade; and finally, from Belgrade, heading south toward Skopje and the Greek border. Taken together, these seem to be pieces of a single long motorway running through the long north-south axis of the country. The second main road on this axis is the well-engineered highway along the Dalmatian coast from Trieste to the Albanian border. Because of the Dinaric barrier, major highway links between these two main lines are scarce. Two lesser highways do run inland from the coast's major cities, Split and Dubrovnik. But beyond the mountains in the valleys of the Sava and Danube, the network of major roads is more extensive.

Whenever we think of Yugoslavia, we recall the lovely Dalmatian coast in Croatia, a narrow strip squeezed between the mountains and the Adriatic Sea. Here porous limestone rock, called "karstic," does not hold water but lets it seep through to form subterranean caves and rivers. As you move south along the coast, this white rock becomes even more exposed and barren, creating a sharper contrast between land and sea. Building the coastal road in the 1960s could not have been easy along these limestone mountain slopes that fall precipitously into the sea without natural ledges. Rock walls have been built to prevent erosion and to keep the highway in place, but it is still subject to a fierce mountain wind, the bora, that sometimes (allegedly) blows cars over the edge into the sea. Clusters of islands just off the coast are resort centers; some can be reached by causeway, others by ferry.

Slovenia, the northern part of Yugoslavia, is, of course, mountainous, its high Julian Alps northwest of Lubljana impinging on the Italian and Austrian borders. A road network links the region's centers for both summer and winter recreation. Mount Triglav, at 2,864 meters (9,394 feet), is the highest peak in Yugoslavia.

Farther south, inland Croatia contains Plitvice National Park, a haven of sixteen crystal lakes interconnected with rivers, terraces, and cascades. From Croatia's capital, Zagreb, east through Vojvodina to Belgrade in Serbia, the long Sava River valley provides a strip of flat land before it joins the larger Danube. This route is the main line from western and northern Europe to Turkey and the Middle East and is often busy with heavy traffic. Southern Serbia and the other republics of the south—Montenegro, Kosovo, and Macedonia—return to the mountains that are the hallmark of the country as a whole. They contain a number of national parks along the Albanian and Greek borders and two large lakes near Ohrid.

ROAD CONDITIONS

Some roads in Yugoslavia have been rebuilt, and in the interior the highways are being upgraded to two-lane highways. Those in the northwest are usually of asphalt. Secondary roads, frequented by people and animals, can be slow.

The coastal road is in good condition, but tourists complain about the lack of guardrails against steep drops into the sea. Roads in the mountainous hinterland can be impassable in winter.

HIGHWAY SIGNS

Road signs correspond to international standards, and words on road signs are written in the Latin alphabet.

DRIVING REGULATIONS

• Vehicles must not exceed the prescribed speed limits. The speed limit in towns is 60 kph/37 mph, and outside towns on motorways 120 kph/74 mph, on roads reserved for motor vehicles 100 kph/62 mph, and on all other roads 80 kph/50 mph.
• Public transport and vehicles specially marked for children have right-of-way when pulling out onto the main road.
• Safety belts are compulsory.
• Children under twelve years of age and intoxicated persons may not ride in the front seat.

- The red-reflector warning triangle is compulsory.
- Vehicles drive on the right-hand side of the road, or in the right-hand lane if there are several lanes. The other lanes are to be used for passing.
- In towns all lanes may be used by all vehicles, except those traveling less than 40 kph/25 mph, which must stay in the right-hand lane.
- In conditions of poor visibility, both day and night, vehicles must keep their lights on dim.
- Drivers may not overtake or pass a line of cars, regardless of whether they are moving or at a standstill.
- Drivers must have a Green or Blue Insurance Card, which can also be obtained from Yugoslav insurance companies at border crossings.
- All vehicles must carry a first-aid kit and a replacement set of light bulbs.

PARKING

Parking meters are in use in some towns. Motorists may use the time left on a meter without further payment.

EMERGENCY INFORMATION

Road-assistance service may be reached by dialing 987.

GASOLINE STATIONS

Foreign visitors can buy gas at a discount with coupons sold at border crossings, tourist bureaus, and the Automobile Association of Yugoslavia offices in major cities. They may also be purchased from some banks and travel agencies abroad.

Stations on main roads often remain open day and night. On other roads the stations are sometimes quite far apart.

Unleaded gasoline is labeled BMB 95.

INTERNATIONAL ROAD SIGNS

REGULATORY SIGNS

PRIORITY ROAD SIGNS

Priority for
oncoming traffic

Priority over
oncoming traffic

Give way

Stop

Priority road

End of
priority road

MANDATORY SIGNS

Pass this side

Direction to be followed

Compulsory
roundabout

Compulsory footpath

Compulsory
cycle track

Compulsory track for
horseback riders

End of compulsory
minimum speed

Compulsory
minimum speed

Snow chains
compulsory

PROHIBITORY OR RESTRICTIVE SIGNS

Closed to all vehicles in both directions

No entry

No entry for any power-driven vehicle except two-wheeled motorcycles without side cars

No entry for any power-driven vehicle drawing a trailer other than a semi-trailer or a single-axle trailer

No entry for goods vehicles

No entry for mopeds

No entry for cycles

No entry for motorcycles

No entry for vehicles carrying more than a certain amount of explosives or readily inflammable substances

No entry for vehicles carrying more than a certain quantity of substances liable to cause water pollution

No entry for power-driven agricultural vehicles

No entry for hand carts

No entry for animal-drawn vehicles

No entry for pedestrians

No entry for vehicles having an overall height exceeding __ meters (__ feet)

No entry for vehicles having an overall width exceeding __ meters (__ feet)

No entry for vehicles or combination of vehicles exceeding __ meters (__ feet) in length

No entry for vehicles having a weight exceeding __ tons on one axle

No entry for vehicles exceeding ____ tons laden weight

Driving of vehicles less than__ meters (__ feet) apart prohibited

PROHIBITORY OR RESTRICTIVE SIGNS

No entry for power-driven vehicles

No entry for power-driven vehicles or animal-drawn vehicles

No left turn

No right turn

No U-turns

Maximum speed limited to the figure indicated

Overtaking prohibited by goods vehicles

Overtaking prohibited

End of all local prohibitions imposed on moving vehicles

End of speed limit

End of prohibition overtaking

Passing without stopping prohibited

Use of audible warning devices prohibited

Parking prohibited

Standing and parking prohibited

Alternate parking: prohibited on odd number dates

Alternate parking: prohibited on even number dates

Limited duration parking zone

Exit from the limited duration parking zone

INFORMATIVE SIGNS

USEFUL INFORMATION SIGNS

Tourist
information

Filling station

Telephone

Restaurant

Hotel or motel

Refreshments
or cafeteria

Picnic site

Camping site

Starting point
for walk

Trailer site

Camping and
trailer site

Youth hostel

Hospital

Hospital

USEFUL INFORMATION SIGNS

First aid station

Breakdown
service

Parking

One way

One way

Road for
motor vehicles

End of road for
motor vehicles

Motorway

End of
motorway

No through road

Tramway stop

Bus stop

Road open or closed

Car-sleeper train

Car-carrier train

Ferry

ADVANCE DIRECTION SIGNS

Advance
diversion sign

No through road

General case

General case

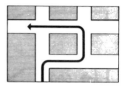

Route to be followed
for left turn

Layout of
priority road

Lane preselection
at intersection

Direction
to airfield

Direction to
a place

Direction to a
youth hostel

Direction to a
camping site

Beginning of
a built-up area

End of a
built-up area

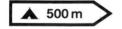

Confirmatory
sign

Pedestrian
crossing

WARNING SIGNS

Dangerous bend

Carriageway
narrows

Carriageway
narrows

Steep ascent or descent:
dangerous descent ___ %

Dangerous bend:
double bend

Dangerous bend:
left bend

Uneven road: dip

Uneven road: hump
bridge or ridge

Uneven road:
bad condition

Road leads on to
quay or river bank

Swing bridge

Children

Pedestrian
crossing

Falling rocks

Loose gravel

Slippery road

Airfield

Light signals

Road works

Animal crossing

WARNING SIGNS

Cattle crossing

Cyclists

Level crossing:
without gates

Level crossing: with
gates or staggered
half gates

Other dangers

Two-way traffic

Cross wind

Approach to
intersection

Approach to intersection:
general priority rule

Approach to intersec-
tion: roundabout

Approach to intersec-
tion: merging traffic

Approach to inter-
section: side road

Location of level crossing
without gate or barrier:
one track

Location of level crossing
without gate or barrier:
at least two tracks

Intersection with
tramway line

Count-down
posts

MAPS OF SELECT CITIES

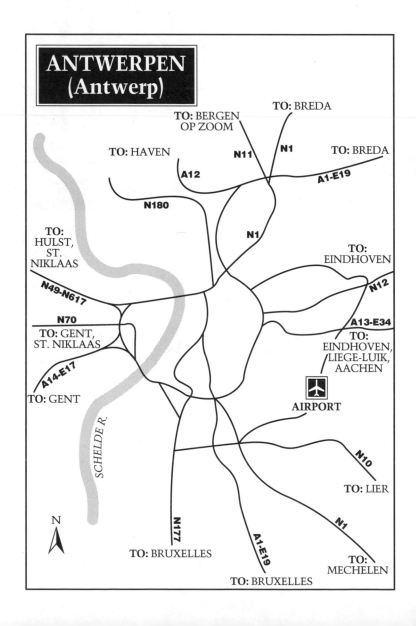

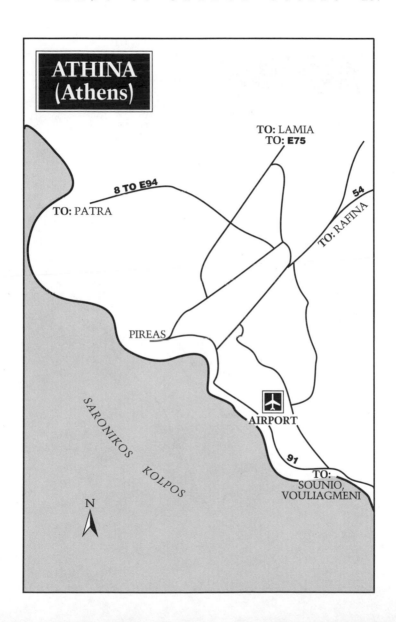

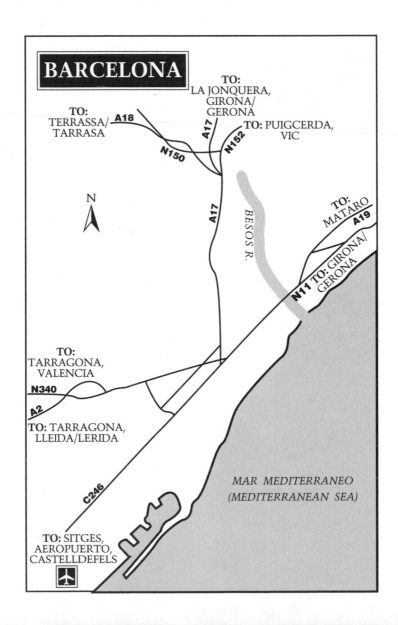

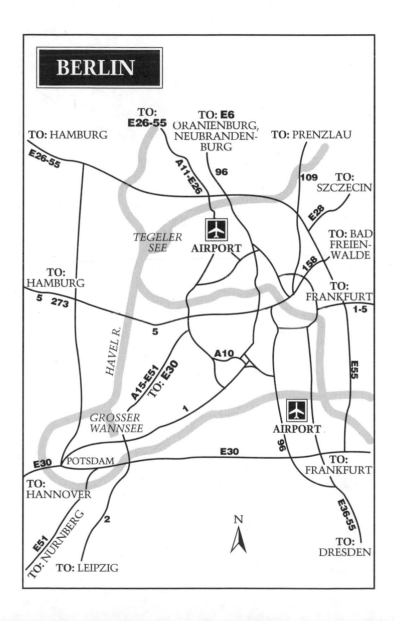

BERLIN

TO: HAMBURG

TO:
E26-55

TO: E6
ORANIENBURG,
NEUBRANDEN-
BURG

TO: PRENZLAU

E26-55

A11-E26

96

109

TO:
SZCZECIN

E28

TO: BAD
FREIEN-
WALDE

TEGELER
SEE

AIRPORT

158

TO:
HAMBURG

TO:
FRANKFURT

5   273

1-5

5

HAVEL R.

A10

A15-E51
TO: E30

E55

1

GROSSER
WANNSEE

AIRPORT

E30

POTSDAM

E30

96

TO:
FRANKFURT

TO:
HANNOVER

E36-55

E51

TO: NURNBERG

2

N

TO:
DRESDEN

TO: LEIPZIG

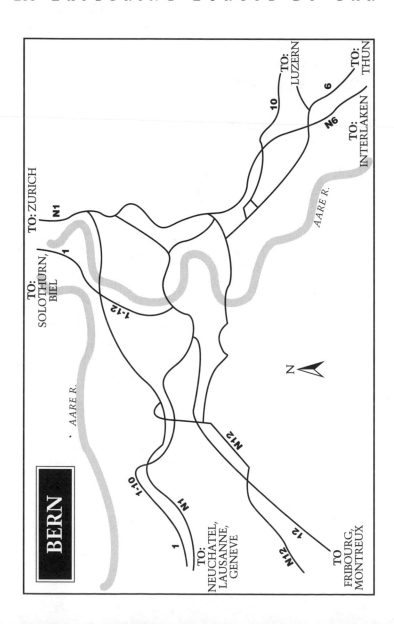

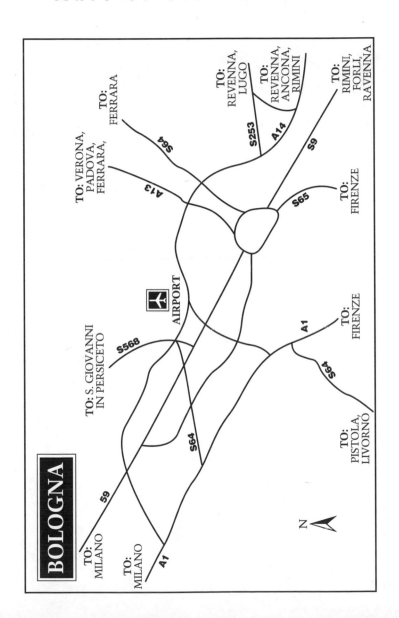

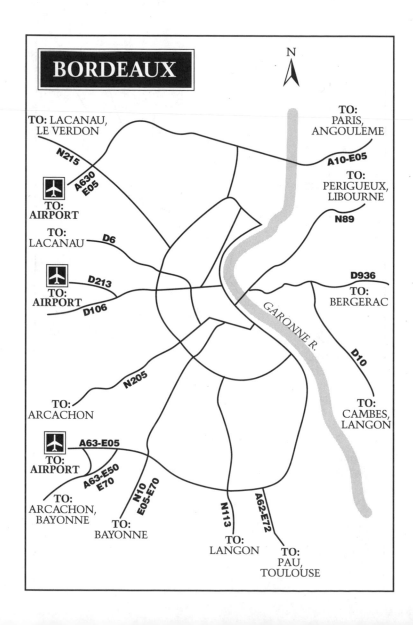

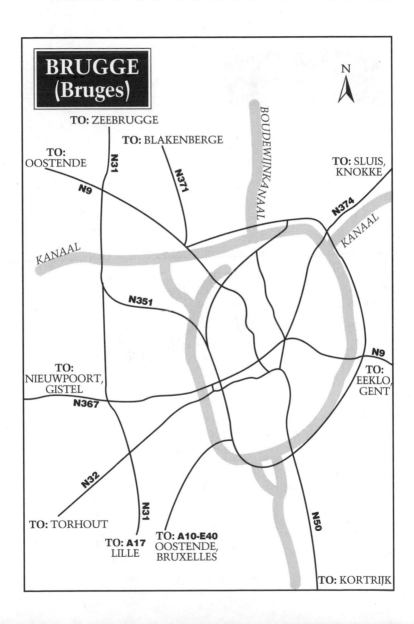

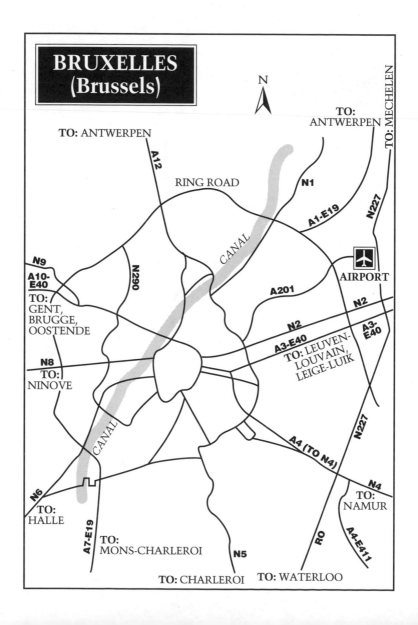

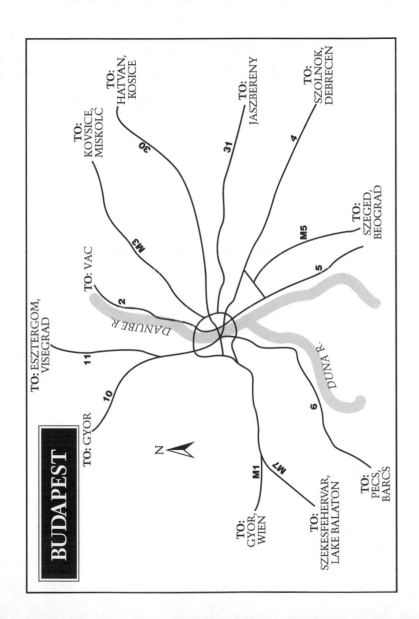

BUDAPEST

TO: GYOR
10
11
TO: ESZTERGOM, VISEGRAD
2
TO: VAC
DANUBE R.
M3
TO: KOVSICE, MISKOLC
30
TO: HATVAN, KOSICE
31
TO: JASZBERENY
4
TO: SZOLNOK, DEBRECEN
M5
TO: SZEGED, BEOGRAD
5
DUNA R.
6
TO: PECS, BARCS
N
M1
M7
TO: GYOR, WIEN
TO: SZEKESFEHERVAR, LAKE BALATON

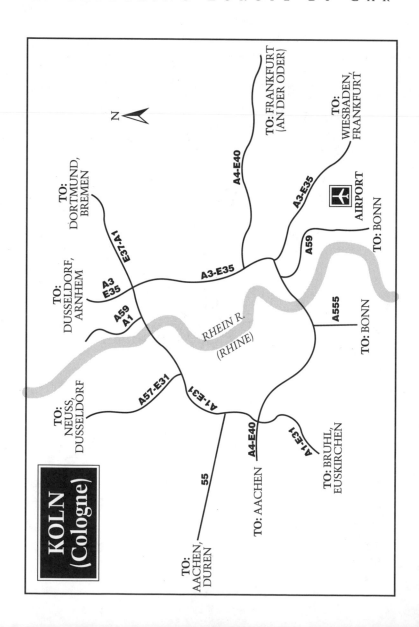

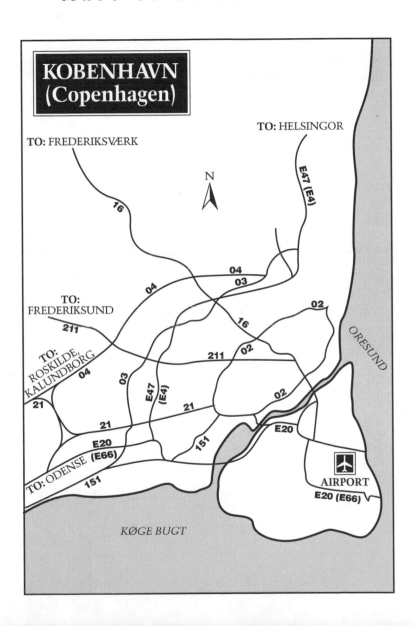

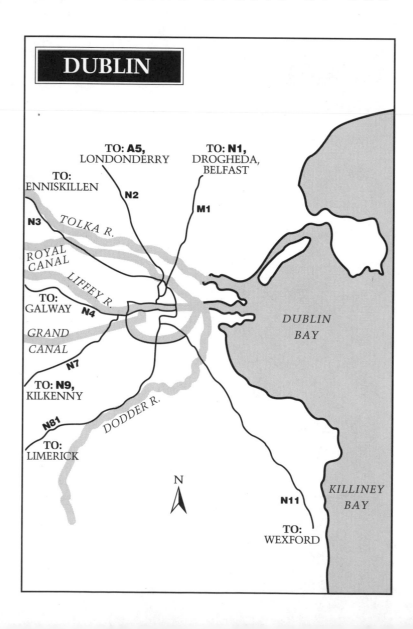

DUBLIN

TO: **A5,** LONDONDERRY

TO: **N1,** DROGHEDA, BELFAST

TO: ENNISKILLEN

N2

M1

N3

TOLKA R.

ROYAL CANAL

LIFFEY R.

TO: GALWAY **N4**

GRAND CANAL

N7

TO: **N9,** KILKENNY

N81

DODDER R.

TO: LIMERICK

DUBLIN BAY

N

KILLINEY BAY

N11

TO: WEXFORD

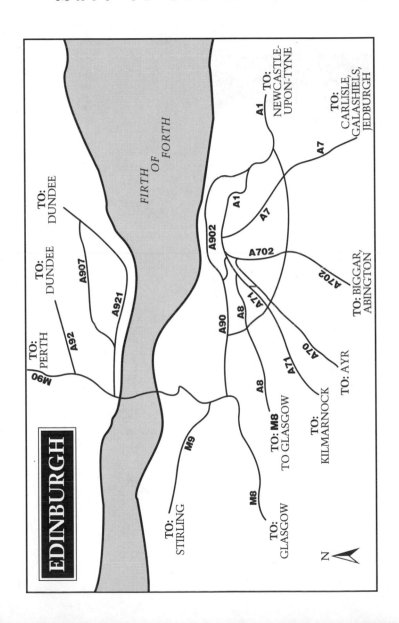

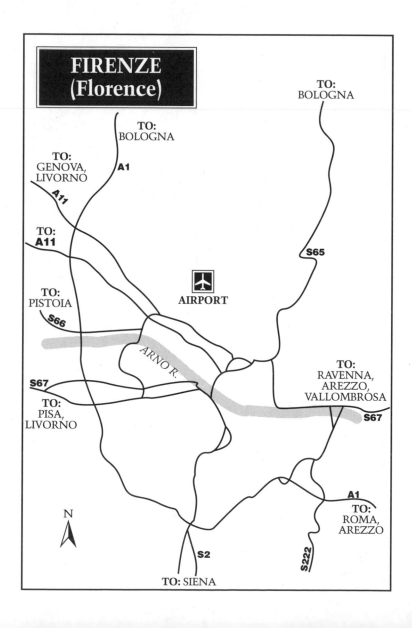

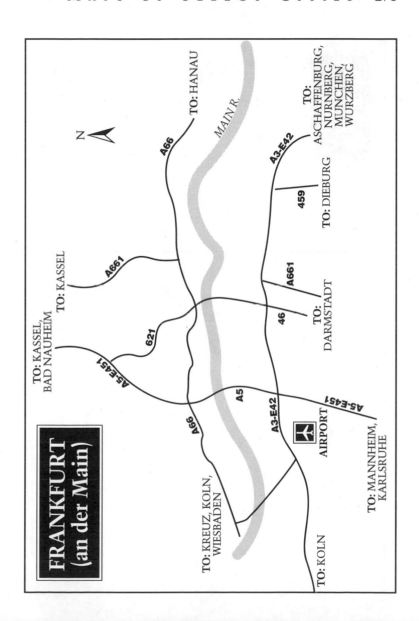

FRANKFURT (an der Main)

N

MAIN R.

TO: HANAU

TO: ASCHAFFENBURG, NURNBERG, MUNCHEN, WURZBERG

A66

A3-E42

TO: DIEBURG

459

TO: KASSEL

A661

A661

TO: DARMSTADT

TO: KASSEL, BAD NAUHEIM

621

46

A5-E451

TO: KASSEL, BAD NAUHEIM

A66

A5

A3-E42

A5-E451

AIRPORT

TO: KREUZ, KOLN, WIESBADEN

TO: MANNHEIM, KARLSRUHE

TO: KOLN

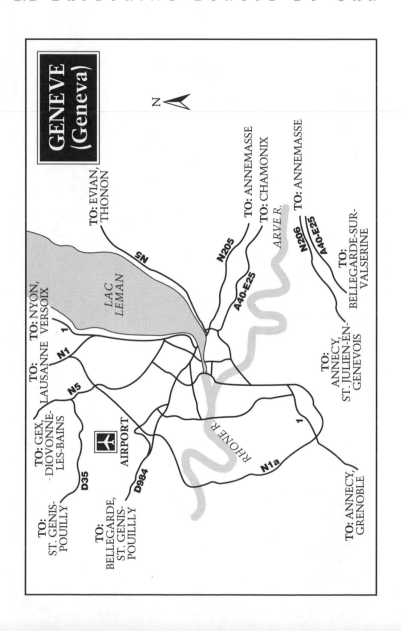

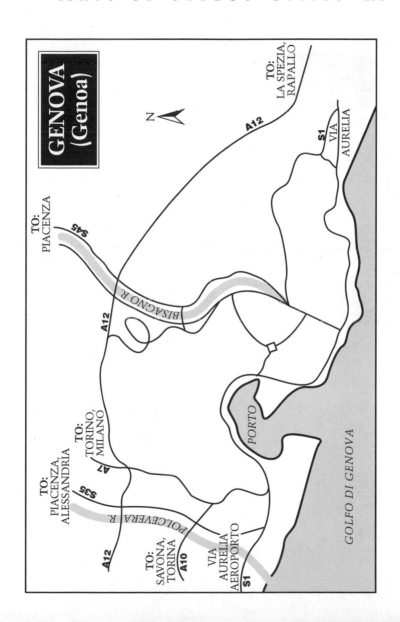

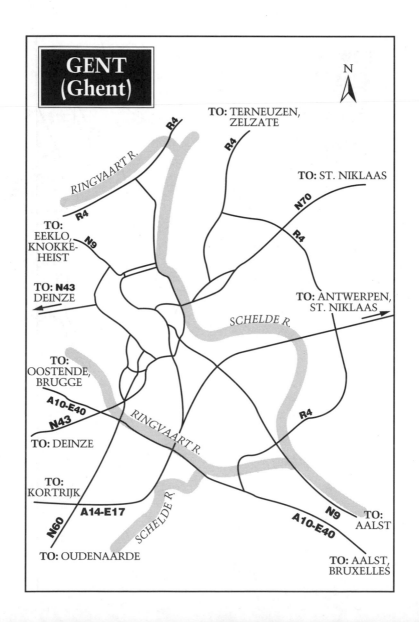

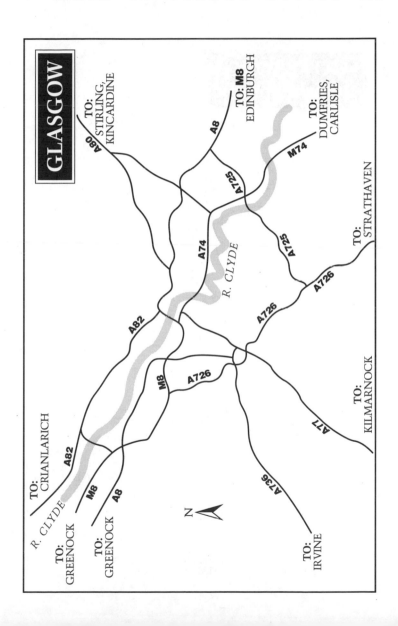

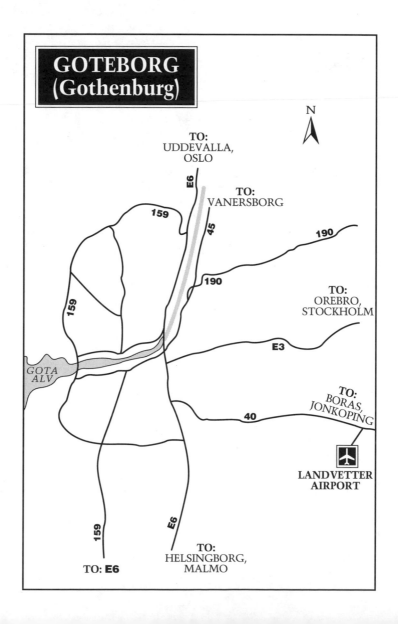

GOTEBORG
(Gothenburg)

N

TO:
UDDEVALLA,
OSLO

E6

TO:
VANERSBORG

159

45

190

159

190

TO:
OREBRO,
STOCKHOLM

159

E3

GOTA
ALV

TO:
BORAS,
JONKOPING

40

LANDVETTER
AIRPORT

159

E6

TO:
HELSINGBORG,
MALMO

TO: E6

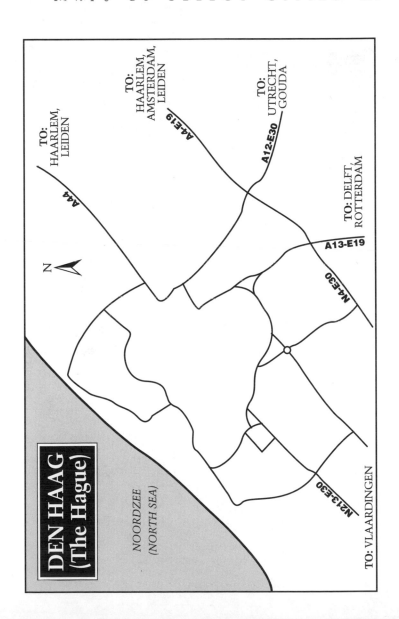

DEN HAAG
(The Hague)

NOORDZEE
(NORTH SEA)

TO:
HAARLEM,
LEIDEN

TO:
HAARLEM,
AMSTERDAM,
LEIDEN

A44

A4-E19

TO:
UTRECHT,
GOUDA

A12-E30

TO: DELFT,
ROTTERDAM

A13-E19

N4-E30

N

TO: VLAARDINGEN

N213-E30

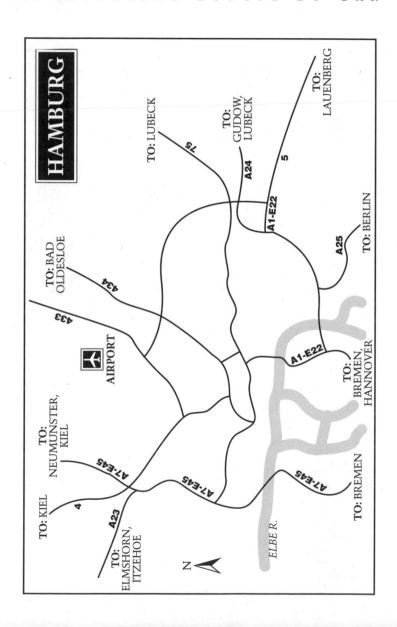

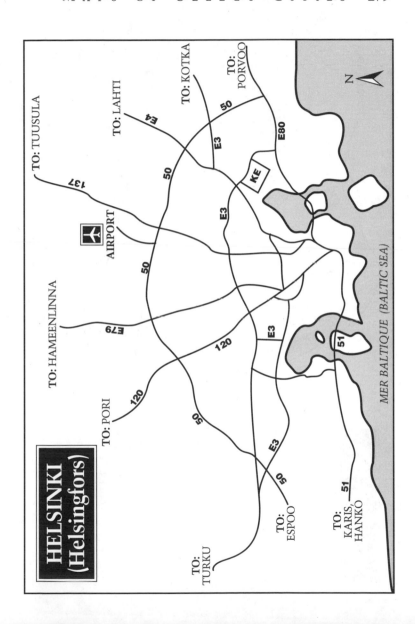

HELSINKI (Helsingfors)

TO: TUUSULA

TO: LAHTI

TO: KOTKA

TO: PORVOO

N

137

E4

50

50

E3

E80

KE

AIRPORT

E3

TO: HAMEENLINNA

E79

E3

120

TO: PORI

120

51

MER BALTIQUE (BALTIC SEA)

50

TO: ESPOO

E3

50

TO: TURKU

TO: KARIS, HANKO

51

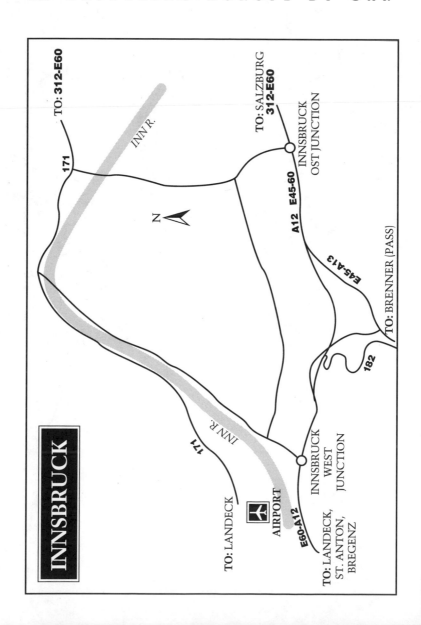

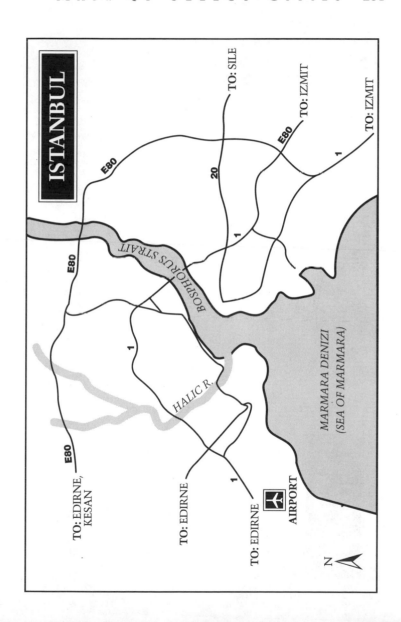

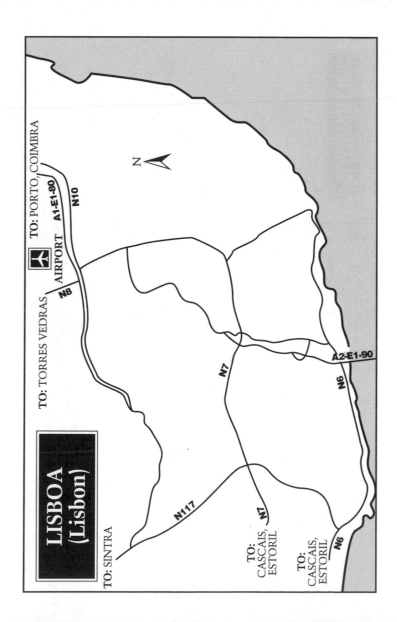

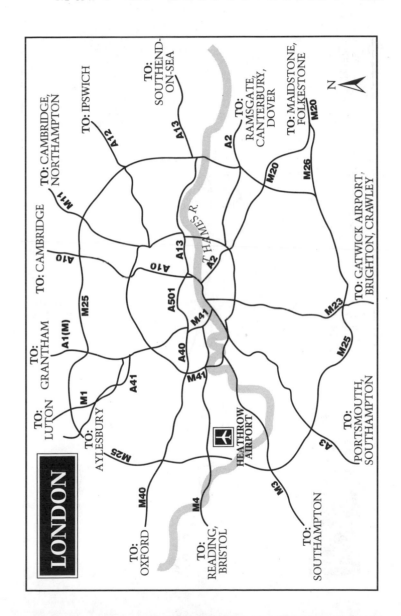

LONDON

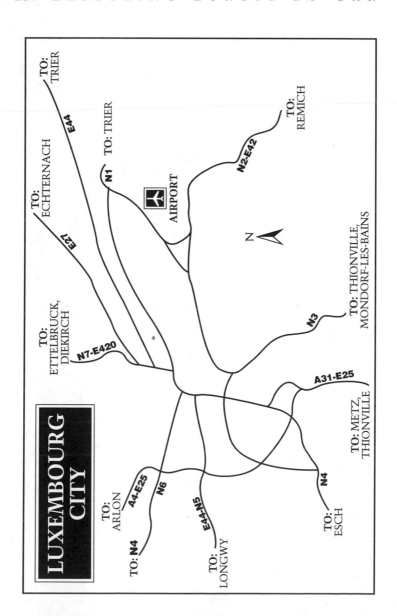

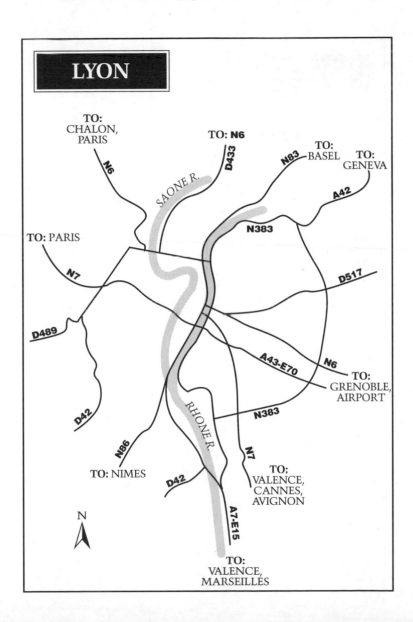

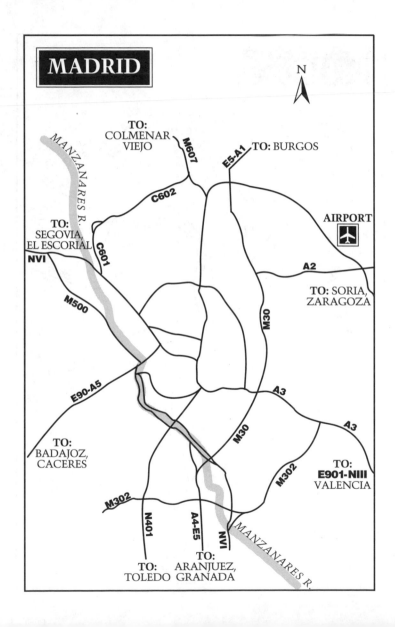

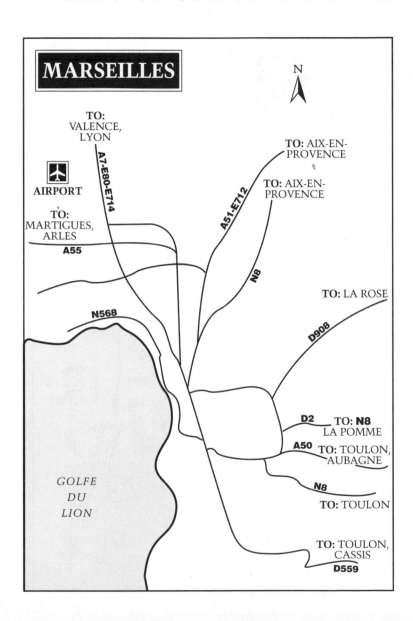

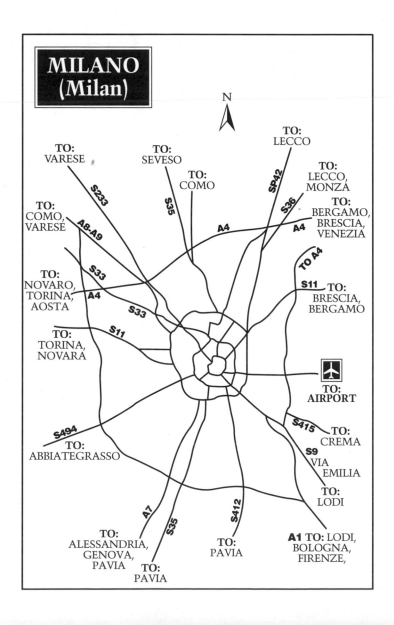

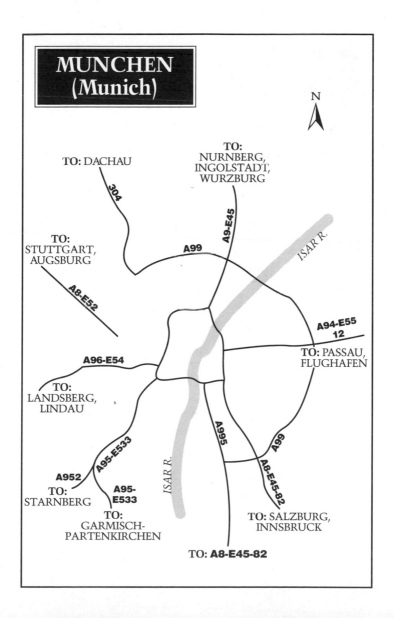

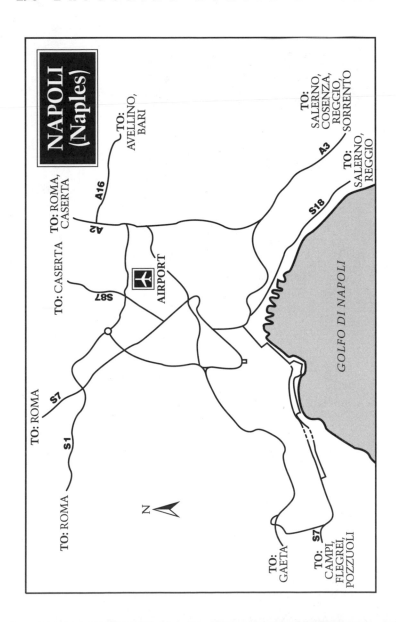

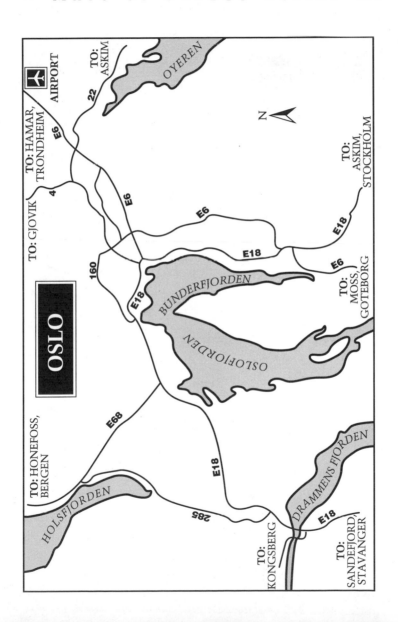

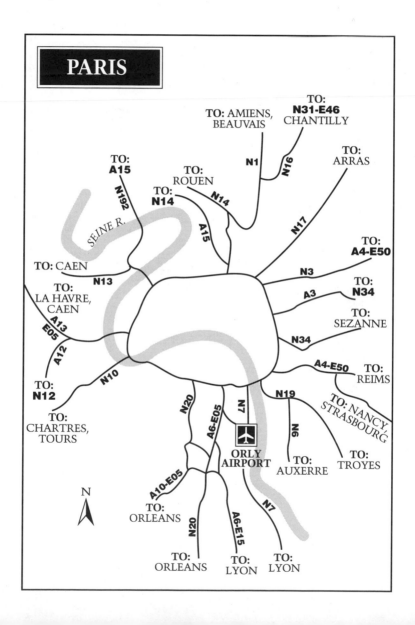

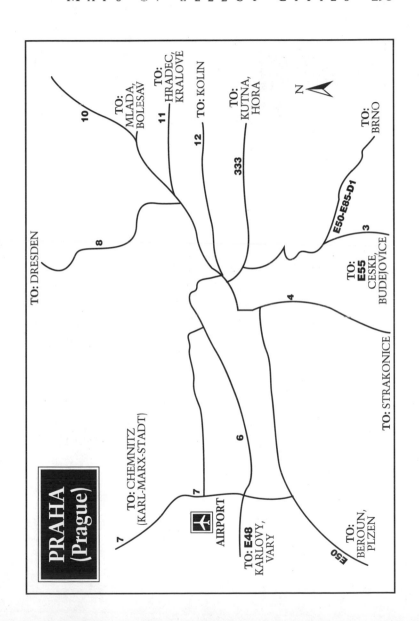

PRAHA (Prague)

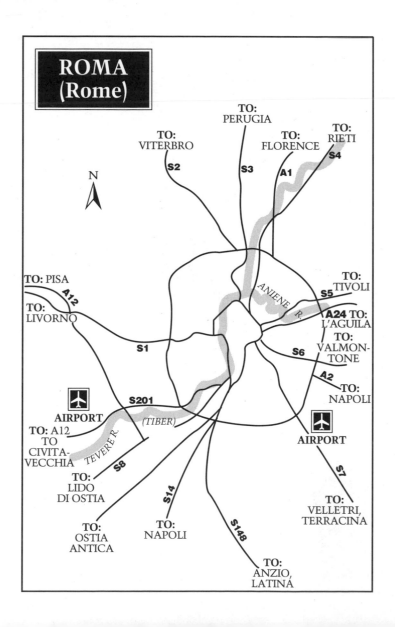

ROMA
(Rome)

N

TO:
PERUGIA

TO:
VITERBRO

TO:
FLORENCE

TO:
RIETI

S2

S3

A1

S4

TO: PISA

A12

TO:
LIVORNO

ANIENE R.

TO:
TIVOLI

S5

A24 TO:
L'AGUILA

S1

TO:
VALMON-
TONE

S6

A2

TO:
NAPOLI

AIRPORT

S201

TO: A12
TO
CIVITA-
VECCHIA

(TIBER)

TEVERE R.

AIRPORT

TO:
LIDO
DI OSTIA

S8

S14

S7

TO:
OSTIA
ANTICA

TO:
NAPOLI

S148

TO:
VELLETRI,
TERRACINA

TO:
ANZIO,
LATINA

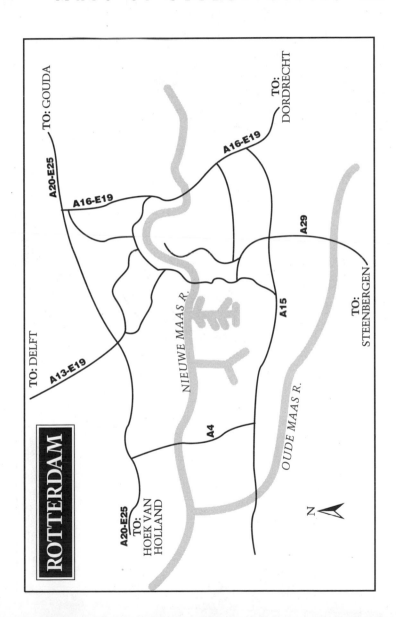

ROTTERDAM

TO: GOUDA

A20-E25

A16-E19

TO: DELFT

A13-E19

A16-E19

TO: DORDRECHT

A29

A15

TO: STEENBERGEN

NIEUWE MAAS R.

OUDE MAAS R.

A4

A20-E25
TO:
HOEK VAN
HOLLAND

N

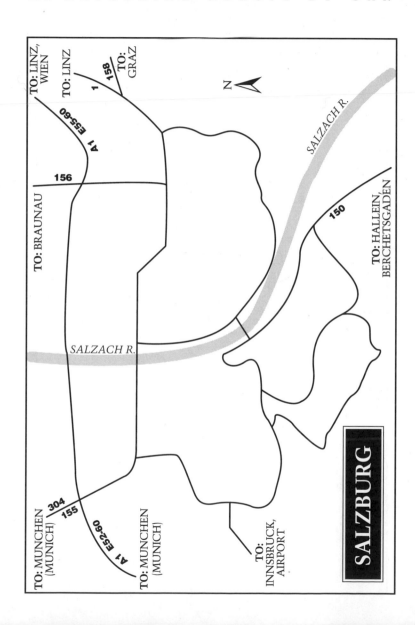

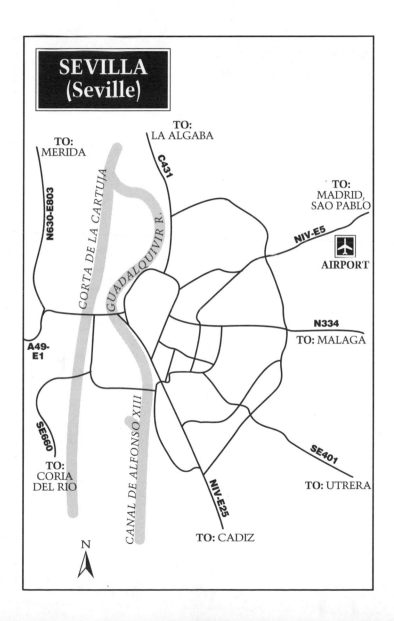

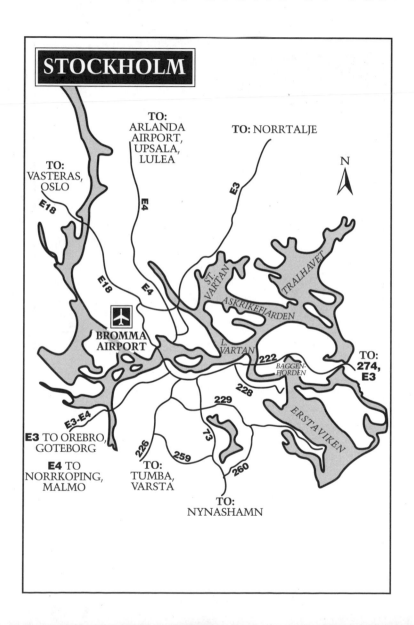

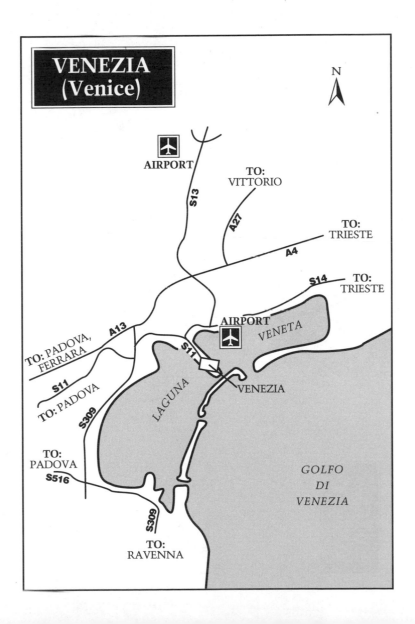

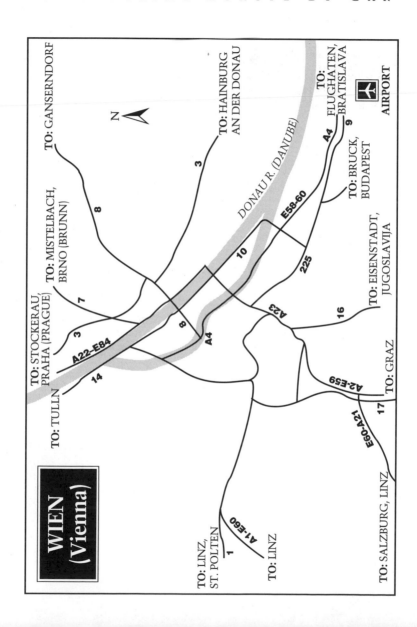

WIEN (Vienna)

N

TO: GANSERNDORF

TO: MISTELBACH, BRNO (BRUNN)

TO: STOCKERAU, PRAHA (PRAGUE)

TO: TULLN

TO: HAINBURG AN DER DONAU

DONAU R. (DANUBE)

TO: FLUGHATEN, BRATISLAVA

AIRPORT

TO: BRUCK, BUDAPEST

TO: EISENSTADT, JUGOSLAVIJA

TO: GRAZ

TO: LINZ, ST. POLTEN

TO: LINZ

TO: SALZBURG, LINZ

3

8

7

3

A22-E84

14

8

A4

10

E58-60

225

A23

16

A2-E59

17

E60-A21

A1-E60

1

9

A4

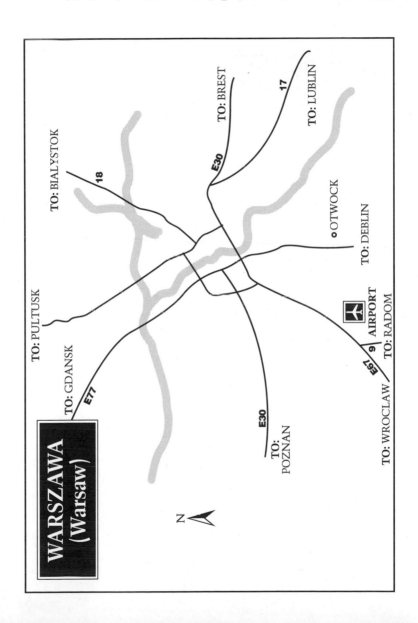

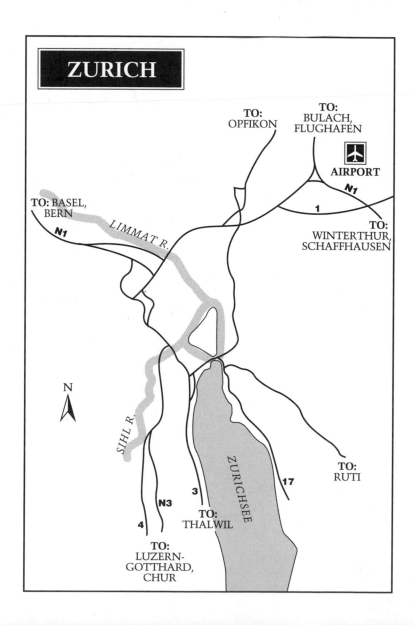

ZURICH

TO: OPFIKON

TO: BULACH, FLUGHAFEN

AIRPORT

N1

TO: BASEL, BERN

N1

LIMMAT R.

1

TO: WINTERTHUR, SCHAFFHAUSEN

N

SIHL R.

ZURICHSEE

TO: RUTI

17

N3

3

TO: THALWIL

4

TO: LUZERN-GOTTHARD, CHUR

APPENDIX

ITINERARY GUIDE

Date	Km/Mi	Hours	City/Town	Notes

WEIGHTS AND MEASURES
CONVERSION TABLES

Length/Kilometers to Miles
(1 kilometer or 1,000 meters = .621 miles)

Kilometers	Miles	Kilometers	Miles
1	0.6	15	9.3
2	1.2	20	12.4
3	1.9	30	18.6
4	2.5	40	24.9
5	3.1	50	31.0
6	3.7	60	37.3
7	4.4	70	43.5
8	5.0	80	49.7
9	5.6	90	55.9
10	6.2	100	62.1

Length/Meters to Feet
(1 meter = 3.28 feet or 39.37 inches)

Meters	Feet	Meters	Feet
1	3.3	7	23.0
2	6.6	8	26.3
3	9.8	9	29.5
4	13.1	10	32.8
5	16.4	100	328.1
6	19.7	1000	3280.8

Area/Hectares to Acres
(1 hectare = 2.5 acres)

Hectares	Acres	Hectares	Acres
0.5	1.2	7	17.3
0.75	1.7	8	19.8
1.00	2.5	9	22.2
2.00	4.9	10	24.7
3.00	7.4	20	49.4
4.00	9.9	30	74.1
5.00	12.4	40	98.8
6.00	14.8	50	123.5

Volume/Liters to Gallons
(3.78 liters = 1 gallon)

Liters	Gallons	Liters	Gallons
1	.26	6	1.59
2	.53	7	1.85
3	.79	8	2.11
4	1.06	9	2.38
5	1.32	10	2.64

Gallons to Liters

Gallons	Liters	Gallons	Liters
1	3.79	6	22.71
2	7.57	7	26.50
3	11.36	8	30.28
4	15.14	9	34.07
5	18.93	10	37.85

Weight/Kilograms to Pounds
(1 kilogram = 2.2 pounds}

Kilograms	Pounds	Kilograms	Pounds
1	2.2	6	13.2
2	4.4	7	15.4
3	6.6	8	17.6
4	8.8	9	19.8
5	11.0	10	22.0

Temperature/Centigrade to Fahrenheit
(–17.7 degrees C. = 0 degrees F.)

Centigrade	Fahrenheit
–17.7	0
–6.6	20
–1.1	30
4.4	40
10.0	50
15.5	60
21.1	70
26.6	80
32.2	90
37.7	100
100.0	212

Tire Pressure

Lbs per sq. inch	Kilos per sq. centimeter
16	1.12
18	1.26
20	1.40
22	1.54
24	1.68
26	1.82
28	1.96
30	2.10
40	2.80
50	3.50
60	4.20

Gradients on Steep Hills

1 in 3 = 30%	1 in 7 = 14%
1 in 4 = 25%	1 in 8 = 12%
1 in 5 = 20%	1 in 9 = 11%
1 in 6 = 16%	1 in 10 = 10%

CLOTHING

U.S.	British	Continental

Women's Dresses and Coats

U.S.	British	Continental
8	10/32	36
10	12/34	38
12	14/36	40
14	16/38	42
16	18/40	44
18	20/42	46
20	22/44	48

(Some items in France and Italy vary from the table.)

Women's Shoes

U.S.	British	Continental
6	4	37
7	5	38
8	6	39
9	7	40

(Some British shoes need to be fitted ½ size larger than listed on table.)

Women's Sweaters and Blouses

U.S.	British	Continental
34	36	40
36	38	42
38	40	44
40	42	46
42	44	48

U.S.	British	Continental

Men's Suits

U.S.	British	Continental
38	38	48
40	40	50
42	42	52
44	44	54

Men's Shirts

U.S.	British	Continental
14	14	36
14½	14½	37
15	15	38
15½	15½	39
16	16	40
16½	16½	41

Men's Shoes

U.S.	British	Continental
8½	8	42
9½	9	43
10½	10	44
11½	11	45

DRIVING TERMS

ENGLISH	FRENCH	GERMAN	ITALIAN	SPANISH
Battery	batterie	Batterie	Batteria	Bateria
Brake	frein	Bremse	Freno	Freno
Bumper	pare-chocs	Stopstange	Paraurti	Parachoques
Carburetor	carburateur	Vergaser	Carburatore	Carburador
Clutch	Embrayage	Kupplung	Innesto	Embrague
Cylinder head	Culasse	Zylinderkopf	Testata del cilindro	Culata
Differential	différentiel	Differential-getriebe	Differenziale	Diferencial
Disc Brake	Frein à disque	Scheibenbremse	Freno a disco	Freno de disco
Distilled water	Eau distillée	Destilliertes wasser	Acqua distillata	Agua destilada
Distributor	distributeur	Zundverteiler	Distributore di corrente	Distribuidor de encendido
Drive Shaft	Arbre de transmission	Antriebswelle trasmissione	Albero di trasmissione	Arbol de transmision
Dynamo	Dynamo	Dynamo	Dinamo	Dinamo
Engine	Moteur	Motor	Motore	Motor
Exhaust Pipe	Tuyau d'echappementescape	Auspuffrohr	tubo di scappamento	Tubo de escape
Fan Belt	Courroie de ventilateur	Ventilatorriemen	Chinghia del ventilatore	Currea de ventilador
Gasket	Joint	Dichtung	Gassetta	Junta
Gasoline or petrol	Essence	Benzin	Benzina	Gasolina
Gear Box	Boîte de vitesse	Getriebe	Scatola del cambio	Caja de velocidades

Gear Lever	Levier de commande	Ger schalthebel	Leva del cambio	Palanca del cambio
Handbrake	Frein à main	Handbremse	Freno a mano	Freno de mano
Headlight	Phare	Scheinwerfer	Fanale Anteriore	Faro
Horn	Klaxon	Hupe	Tromba	Bocina
Ignition	Allumage	Zundung	Accensione	Encendido
Jack	Cric	Wagenheber	Cricco	Gato
Key	Clef	Schlussel	Chiave	Llave
Lock	Serrure	Schloss	Serratura	Cerradura
Lubricate	Graisser	Schmieren	Lubrificare	Engrasar
Oil	Huile	Ol	Olio	Aceite
Piston and Rings	Piston et segments	Kolben und kolbenringe	Pistone e segmenti	Pistón y segmentos
Puncture	Crevaison	Reifenpanne	Foratura (di pneumatico)	Pinchazo
Radiator	Radiateur	Kuhler	Radiatore	Radiador
Shock Absorber	Amortisseur	Stossdampfer	Ammortizzatore	Amortiguador
Snow Chains	Chaînes antidérapantes	Schneeketten	Catene antisducciolevoli	Cadenas para nieve
Spark Plug	Bougie d'allumage	Zundkerze	Candela d'accensione	Bujia
Speedometer	Indicateur de vitesse	Geschwindigkeitmesser	Tachimetro	Velocimetro
Starter	Démarreur	Starter	Messa in moto	Arranque
Tire	Pneu	Reifen	Gomma	Neumático
Valve	Soupape	Ventil	Valvola	Valvula
Wheel	Roue	Rad	Ruota	Rueda
Windshield	Pare-brise	Windschutzscheibe	Parabrezza	Parabrisas

TRIP EXPENSE RECORD

Date	Transport	Lodging	Meals	Entertainment	Telephone	Tips	Other

TIME ZONES

Eastern Standard Time is five hours behind Greenwich Mean Time; Britain, Ireland, and Portugal are all on GMT. Western European countries, including Czechoslovakia, Hungary, Spain, and Yugoslavia use Central European Time: one hour ahead of GMT. Eastern countries, in addition to Finland, Greece, and Turkey function two hours ahead of GMT. Daylight Savings Time will set clocks an hour ahead in the spring; they return to GMT in the fall. Such changes do not occur, however, on the same day throughout Europe. It is wise to check ahead when traveling during these periods of suspected change in spring and fall. Most countries use the twenty-four-hour clock to avoid confusion between morning and evening.

INTERNATIONAL DIRECT-DIALING CODES

The procedure for dialing is to first dial the "dial-out" code which is found in the front of all phone books (for example, the dial-out code for the United States is 011; for Great Britain it is 010.) Then dial the code for the country to be called, then the city code (omitting any initial 0 or 9—except for France, where the 5 or 16 should be omitted; and the United States and Canada, where the full city code is dialed.)

Country Codes

Austria 43, Belgium 32, Czechoslovakia 42, Denmark 45, Finland 358, France 33, Germany 49, Great Britain 44, Greece 30, Hungary 36, Republic of Ireland 353, Northern Ireland 44, Italy 39, Luxembourg 352, The Netherlands 31, Norway 47, Poland 48, Portugal 351, Spain 34, Sweden 46, Switzerland 41, Turkey 90, Yugoslavia 38

COUNTRY SYMBOLS

A	Austria
B	Belgium
CS	Czechoslovakia
DK	Denmark
GB	England, Scotland, Wales
SF	Finland
F	France
D	Germany
GR	Greece
H	Hungary
IRL	Ireland, Republic of
I	Italy
L	Luxembourg
NL	Netherlands
N	Norway
PL	Poland
P	Portugal
E	Spain
S	Sweden
CH	Switzerland
TR	Turkey
YU	Yugoslavia

INDEX

Note: Page numbers in italics indicate country maps